k 1
s/
on

sful
ess
with

ment

Hallmark 2
Customerising

HALLMARK (*höl-mg:k*) *n* 1. A mark of authenticity or excellence. 2. An outstanding feature ˜*vb.* 3. *(tr)* To stamp with as if a Hallmark (after Goldsmiths Hall in London).

Hallmark 3
Partnering

k 4
ity

The Hallmarks for
Successful Business
Survival – Change – Growth

This book is dedicated to my parents Eileen and Joseph Hall, who taught me many of the important things that I needed to know.

The Hallmarks for
Successful Business

Survival – Change – Growth

Practical Hallmarks
for the Independent Company

David Hall

MERCURY

First published in 1992
by Mercury Books
Gold Arrow Publications Limited,
862 Garratt Lane, London SW17 0NB

Set in Garamond by TecSet Limited
Printed and bound in Great Britain by
Bookcraft (Bath) Limited, Midsomer Norton, Avon

British Library Cataloguing in Publication Data is available
ISBN 1–85251–166–4

Preface

This book is for the owner or management of small and medium-sized independent companies. It is full of powerful ideas, which you can use to develop your business and increase your success. This is *not* a textbook; it is a guide to business success. Think of it as a book which you, the reader, and I, the author, are writing together. Make it *your* book. You can do this by taking *action* in your business as a result of reading this book.

To help you, I have identified six factors by which a business can be analysed, and called these 'Hallmarks'. For a start, take out your diary. Identify any internal meetings, cross out the least important and replace them with visits to key customers.

Your aim in these meetings with customers is to help them identify current problems which can be resolved by working in partnership with you. Why should you bother doing this? Quite simply, because their problems are your opportunities.

That is an example of the ideas in this book and the style in which they are offered. Keep on reading for many more, and stamp the Hallmarks of success on your business.

HALLMARK *n.* 1 A mark of authenticity or excellence. 2 An outstanding feature. *vb.* 3 *(tr)* To stamp with as if a hallmark (after Goldsmiths Hall in London).

Acknowledgements

This book is about applying learning. I learned that writing a book requires collaboration with many people.

Thank you most of all to the companies who allowed us to learn from their experiences, and to Dinah Bennett at Durham University Business School (DUBS) who did an excellent job on the original research.

Thank you also to Mike Pedler for editing the book, for taking off the rough edges; to Simon Haslam who encouraged me and added real value to the ideas in the book; to my colleagues in the David Hall Partnership (DHP), who provided many of the examples and anecdotes; to my friends at DUBS, including Alan Gibb and Tim Atterton who provided much of the substance; to Bill Furness of British Coal Enterprise and Gordon Nicholson of Regional Enterprise Unit of Training Employment and Education Department, who co-sponsored the research, and to Gerry Egan who provided the idea of models of management to illustrate complex ideas in a simple manner; to Jack Cockburn, my erudite English adviser; and to Karen Simpson who typed the manuscript.

Contents

Introduction

The aims of this book are:

1. *To help businesses develop successfully, and to sustain that development long-term.*
2. *To pass on Hallmarks for success from actual experience of successful businesses.*
3. *To provide practical ways of using these Hallmarks and add value to your own company.*
4. *To enable support agencies to provide effective help to developing companies.*

What is this Book *really* About?

This book is about how successful independent companies with turnovers of up to £20 million develop and the lessons they learn in the process. These lessons are translated into practical step-by-step guidelines to enable you to achieve similar success. This book is about:

- *How to develop a continuously successful business;*
- *How to generate new business;*
- *How to position your business so that you can charge a premium price;*
- *How to create a sustainable competitive advantage;*
- *How to grow with minimum risk and sleep easily in your bed;*
- *How to ride the waves of boom and bust periods in the economy;*
- *How to become the recognized market leader;*
- *How to become the role model in your industry sector – in other words, 'the best';*

- *How to develop other people so that the business is less dependent on you for its success.*

What it Is not About

It does not address production, personnel, or finance. These are important areas for development, but in my experience finding and keeping enough customers is the first and most important step to success.

With enough customers, these other areas can provide some nice problems for you to tackle next, but this book is about business development through market development.

Hallmarks is not a Magic Formula

This book spells out some Hallmarks to guide you to success, but it does not provide a magic formula. Firstly, Hallmarks need to be tailored to your business, because the route to success depends upon your company's particular circumstances. Secondly, today's success formula may have the opposite effect in a different environment tomorrow. Finally, each business needs to craft its own recipe for success.

Hallmarks are the characteristic features consistently found in successful independent companies. They are not blueprints – you cannot simply copy what others have done. You have to think out how you can stamp the Hallmarks on your own unique business. The Hallmarks contained in this book will help you by providing the basis for assessing, designing, and running the marketing of your business.

Why Was this Book Written?

I have been working with your kind of company over the last ten years and, along with like-minded others, had become dissatisfied with the support and help available to enable them to develop effectively.

- *In the UK, we need to produce more successful businesses, particularly in manufacturing, to maintain a healthy economy.*
- *Our entry into Europe is exposing many UK businesses to aggressive competition for which they are not prepared.*
- *Despite their importance to the UK economy (70 per cent of the labour force works for enterprises employing less than 500 people, making up 30 per cent of GDP), these independent businesses receive very little support, training, or attention. For example, they only merit a junior minister at the DTI (despite the commitment to enterprise development).*

What Is the Potential?

- *In independent companies real dynamism and innovation are often to be found, and it is in them that the big businesses of the future will be built. In the past ten years manufacturing output in the UK has increased by 4 per cent, while consumer spending has increased by 40 per cent. This clearly represents a major opportunity for UK businesses to obtain a share of this increased spend currently being taken by imports.*
- *Many independents find it hard to change or grow. Because they are keen to retain their independence they are reluctant to borrow or give up equity. Hardest of all is building the management team, delegating operational control, and finding successors.*
- *Consequently, relatively few companies are consistently successful over a period of five years or more.*

Amid the welter of published advice on business success, why is this book important?

- *Because most support for marketing and business development is based on big company models.*
- *Because marketing support tends to be administrative – for example, how to obtain an export licence. The major problems are to do with getting orders, making customer contacts, and meeting the right people.*

All this adds up to a mismatch of the needs of independent business and the type of support and help available, so we at the David Hall Partnership, together with Durham Business School, set out to find ways of helping these businesses more effectively. We asked ourselves:

- *How can we help independent businesses which are impatient for success?*
- *What can be learnt from successful companies?*
- *Can we find some principles for success which we can confidently pass on to others?*

This book answers these questions.

Who is David Hall?

My children ask the same question! I run a business and, I suspect like you, work long hours, often spending time away from home. From training and consultancy in major companies I went independent because I was inundated with theory and wanted to get involved in the practice of running a business. I recall walking out of a lecture on marketing at an eminent business school thinking, 'It's not like this in the real world'. I turned my back on my PhD, handed in my notice and started working off the dining-room table. Owner-managers are risk-takers and mavericks, so in for a penny....

David Hall Partnership Ltd (DHP) is a rapidly growing training and consultancy business. We started in 1986 and now employ 50 people. We have experienced for ourselves the adventures of rapid growth, so some of our own experiences are in this book too! We help businesses grow and develop. In 1990 we trained and advised more than 500 businesses, ranging from start-ups to multinationals.

I am a visiting fellow at Durham University Business School. Durham has an international reputation for practical and innovative work with independent businesses. It conducted the research sponsored by DHP, which underpins this book.

Helping businesses to grow and develop is my chosen profession – my job in my business.

Is it Right for you and your Business?

Do any of the following apply to you?

- *You are looking for a way of assessing your business;*
- *You want to develop your business and would appreciate some practical help;*
- *You want to survive, change or grow in business in a systematic manner;*
- *You would like practical learning examples from independent businesses similar to yours;*
- *You want to generate new business;*
- *You want to grow with minimum risk;*
- *You want to increase your prices without losing revenue;*
- *You want to take management more seriously.*

Exactly how Will it Work?

This book is designed to give *you* choices, about how you use it and what actions (if any) you decide to take.

Here is an overview of how the book works:

Pages 9–19 Here we answer some of the important questions you may be considering before getting into the book. – What is the book about? Is it right for me?

Pages 21–29 This section helps you to get the most out of the book by showing you how to gather information in order to assess your business against the Hallmarks we suggest. It also shows you a way to maximize the benefits you can get by reading this book through accelerated learning.

Pages 31–222 Here we show you how to apply the Hallmarks to the development of your business. Each Hallmark is discussed at three levels.

Level 1	*Awareness*	*You understand the process of successful development by reading the text and case studies.*
Level 2	*Assessment*	*You compare your business activities with the success factors using the framework provided.*
Level 3	*Action*	*You formulate actions to develop your own Hallmarks.*

You decide how far you want to go, which factors you want to work on and to what level.

The last part of the book is your 'toolkit', which enables you to work effectively with the Hallmarks.

Toolkit 1 *Shows you how to conduct an internal assessment of your business against the Hallmarks, using a simple questionnaire.*

Toolkit 2 *Sets out exactly how to complete a Customer Perception Survey in order to find out how you are perceived by your customers. This provides the basis for developing your business.*

Toolkit 3   *Provides background reading to the process of problem-seeking/problem-solving to help you to get to grips with the process that is the core of successful business development. The benefits are that you will create more business opportunities than you can handle.*

Toolkit 4   *Describes in detail a business-generating system to ensure you have ample new opportunities.*

Appendix   *Details how the research with the thirty companies in our survey was conducted. This was a substantial research programme, involving a full-time researcher over two years.*

My Definitions of Words and Phrases Used in this Book

Accelerated learning:	*Consciously increasing the quality and quantity of positive learning.*
Core skills:	*What you are really good at.*
Customer delight:	*Surprising customers by the level of service you provide to them personally.*
Customerising:	*Continually delighting customers.*
Framework:	*A summary of the Hallmarks (or outstanding features).*
Hallmarks:	*The outstanding features of a successful business.*
Independent company:	*One which is privately owned with sales from £0.2 m to £20 m annual sales.*
Mission:	*The definition of the business you are in.*
Networking:	*Working with those who can influence your business, e.g. bank managers, signposters, accountants.*
The 'shadow side':	*The undiscussable side of business – politics, culture, etc.*

A successful business: *One which meets the following criteria:*
- *less than 10 years old and now employs 100+ people;*
- *maintained planned profit performance over the period of growth;*
- *became recognized leaders in their market sector.*

Vision: *The future you want.*

The Hallmarks for Success

This book is based on information and learning from three major sources:

1. Research into thirty independent companies. Their experiences provide a number of Hallmarks for success. This section introduces you to these companies and provides an overview of their success routes. Key points are illustrated by examples from the experiences of these companies. Many of the quotations used are reproduced without alteration from recorded interviews.
2. David Hall Partnership has helped over a thousand businesses survive, change and grow. We have identified many lessons from those that have been successful.
3. Finally, my own business has grown profitably from one to fifty people in five years. We have experienced and learned from problems of growth, and are still learning.

The Research Companies

The basis for selecting the businesses for our research was:

- *Small to medium, independent, privately owned businesses;*
- *Turnover range £200,000–£20m;*
- *Manufacturing and service sectors.*

Eighty companies who met the criteria were identified and contacted, and thirty agreed to be involved in the research project.

The principles of success come from their experiences. As they are the stars of the book they deserve to be credited here. The detailed research programme is outlined in the Appendix.

Company	Area of Operation
ABI Electronics	*Electronic test equipment*
Ace	*Conveyor systems*
Bede Scientific	*X-ray diffraction instruments*
Bonas Machine Company	*Weaving machines*
Canford Audio	*Manufacturers of audio and broadcasting equipment*
Chameleon Design	*Decorative mirrors*
Compass Caravans	*Touring caravans*
Cresstale	*Manufacturers of lipstick holders and compacts*
Derwent Valley Foods	*Snack foods*
Electrix Northern	*Stockists and manufacturers of stainless-steel equipment*
Elfab Hughes	*Safety equipment*
Fellowes	*Manufacturer of office supplies*
Great Northern Knitwear	*Men's knitted outer garments*
Higgins	*Potato processing*
Integrated Micro Products	*Multi-user computer systems*
Metro FM	*Broadcasting*
NB Print and Design	*Print and design*
Neat Ideas	*Office supplies by mail order*
Nicholson Seals	*Gaskets and seals*
Osborne Engineering	*Manufacturer of white metal bearings*
Osborne Kay	*Printers*
Panda Supplies	*Protective clothing and equipment*
Paul and Loughran	*Gas compressor manufacturers*
Polydon Industries	*Production engineering*

Shield Engineering	*Precision toolmakers*
South Riding Video	*Maker of video and TV films*
Superior Cleaning Spec-	*Contract cleaning*
ialists	
Tolag	*Manufacturer of defence*
	components
Topline	*Business services*
Tyne Tec	*Access control equipment and*
	alarms

We set out to find what made some of the businesses more successful than others.

What is Success?

Success depends on the aims of the company and the conditions in which it operates. In recessionary times successful companies may be those who manage to stay in business but achieve planned profitability long term. We were looking at companies which had survived, grown or changed throughout the 1970s and 1980s.

Of the thirty successful companies we decided to apply tougher criteria of success in order to divide our samples into three groups:

1. *Fast-growth successful companies;*
2. *Average successful companies;*
3. *Successful mature companies.*

Seven companies fitted our fast growth criteria. This was out of a sample who were all regarded (by us) as successful, but seven had done it much faster. What they had in common was:

- *They are less than ten years old but had grown to over a hundred employees;*
- *They have maintained planned profit performance over the period of growth;*
- *They have become recognized leaders in their market sector.*

What is Development – Growth or Change?

While seven companies were fast growth, employing more than a hundred people, several others had changed successfully. Growth is normally regarded as an increase in sales volume. However, we live in changing times and success can also be seen as the ability to recognize and meet changing customer requirements by adapting the business.

This may not lead automatically to an increase in sales turnover but it often maintains the customer base, leading to a continuation of or increase in profits. We considered successful adaption of the business also to be 'success'.

Findings

Hallmarks By analysing the successful companies we were able to develop a *Framework* for successful business development. The successful businesses all had the Hallmarks of success. They fitted the dictionary definition of 'Hallmark' as an *'outstanding feature'*.

By means of the Framework you can achieve your aim of successful business development. Hallmarks lead you to the achievement of your aim. They are the principles for success for fast growth and successfully changing companies with a long-term future. The Business Development Framework also provides an overview of the research findings.

The Framework presents six Hallmarks as a model that depicts the linkage between them. Implementation as a whole is the way to successful business development.

The Framework is a cycle because:

- *The tasks to be completed are presented as a sequence (although you need to pay attention to them all at once). Start at twelve o'clock with Hallmark 1, Focus/Direction, and work clockwise. Our research suggests that there is a natural, logical order to complete the tasks which it is useful to follow, and there are also pragmatic reasons – for example, you cannot get involved in continual improvements in quality (total quality management) until you have installed BS5750.*

- *You cannot determine what critical resources are required until you have an overall view for the future.*
- *The tasks are obviously dependent on each other. For example, Osborne Engineering used 'Quality' to improve its personality in the eyes of its major customers.*
- *There is no such thing as completing the growth or change task. It is a constant journey.*

Why Hallmarks?

The Hallmarks provide a model for managing which is missing in many businesses. They provide a shared model which gives everyone in the business a roadmap, enabling them to decide their priorities.

Hallmarks also help you to plan and implement change. Many people and companies resist change out of fear. The Hallmarks provide a method of changing beliefs and making change an adventure. They will help you to develop your business providing you are ready to take management seriously.

Focus/Direction: Fashioning and managing the overall focus and direction of the business

The successful companies in our survey all had clear focus and direction, which allowed people to harness their personal energies and add value to the business. Everybody was heading the same way. Few companies had written plans or strategies. Focus and direction were provided by the top team acting as role models for the business overall, the strategies being rolled out by example. This was particularly evident in Derwent Valley Foods, Metro FM and Neat Ideas.

Hallmark 2

Customerising: Continually delighting customers

The successful companies without exception are committed to delighting their customers. Their method is such that we found difficulty in finding a word in the English language to describe it fully. Marketing, for example, was not descriptive enough. These companies focus on customers, not markets. (In the history of business, a market never bought anything.) From top management down they identify with customers, sorting out their problems, providing effective solutions, and building relationships. I felt the ideal process was not really captured by our vocabulary: hence *Customerising*.

Successful companies clearly define their core skills (what they are good at) and stick to them. They grow and develop by leveraging that strength with new customers, often geographically, using a business-generating system. Cresstale, Compass and Ace make solving customers' problems in partnership a priority.

Partnering: **Working in partnership with people who affect the business**

Working in partnership with all the key people who affect the business is a way of life for successful companies. They treat their customers, staff, suppliers, and distributors as partners in their business. This is not a manipulative ploy but a genuine conviction that working in partnership is the way to succeed.

For example, Neat Ideas fitted radios in the cabs of their distributors' vans to help them improve communications. They also encourage their suppliers to join them in their in-company training programmes. Derwent Valley Foods has a company newspaper that is sent to customers, employees, suppliers and distributors.

Hallmark 4

Personality: **The character of the business**

Commitment to a successful company image (external) is achieved through a carefully managed company personality (internal). Company personality is managed through a clear vision that is communicated to everyone, with top management personally providing clear examples to follow.

Successful companies have the look and feel of success. They have a personality and a vitality not seen in other businesses. Their external image is not left to chance. Superior Cleaning Specialists clearly defined their company image, down to the colours of their employees' overalls and the livery of their vehicles. This was one of its main attractions to its biggest customer, British Telecom, because at the time BT was trying to improve its own image with its customers. They ran an advertising campaign emphasising the number of telephone boxes in working order. Superior Cleaning Specialists' clear visible identity added real value to this aim.

Hallmark 5

Quality: **A commitment to providing product quality and customer service**

Quality is the key, both for the product and customer service. Commitment to quality enables successful companies not only to please customers but to charge premium prices for doing so. BS5750 is the norm, not the exception, in these companies, although this is just the starting point.

Superior Cleaning Specialists offers a customised service at a premium price. Derwent Valley Foods has a quality product in superior packaging which allows them to price at three times the industry average. Cresstale focuses on getting quality right for each individual customer. Neat Ideas carries out spot checks on its carriers to ensure distribution meets their quality standards.

These companies do not just go in for 'customer care' but for *customer delight*.

Hallmark 6

Systems: **Establishing systems to provide infor-
            mation empowers people to make key
            decisions**

Some companies have clearly defined what they need to
monitor and control to be successful. As well as being tightly
controlled financially, they monitor key customer indicators
and use the information to make management decisions. The
difference between ordinary businesses and the successful
ones is that most successful companies provide information
to empower people to act rather than control them.

Neat Ideas has reduced telephone ordering waiting time to
three seconds. They take *action* on the information rather
than collect and store it.

The First Step

In order to complete the Hallmarks for your business you need to gather information and take action. This chapter offers some practical tips about using the book, gathering information by which to assess your business, and how to take actions to develop it. The learning model is explained in depth. Finally, it introduces the idea of accelerated learning. How can you maximize your learning and develop your business quickly?

Development model	*Outcome*
Level 1: Awareness	Understanding of the process of successful business development.
Level 2: Assessment	Assess your business against the Hallmarks.
Level 3: Action	What action to take to develop your business.

Level 1: Awareness

Awareness is a basic understanding of how businesses achieved success. In creating awareness I have deliberately avoided theory and jargon and tried to encourage the successful companies to paint pictures for you by telling their own stories. When you read each awareness section try to relate the experience of others to your own business. How could we do that? Could we make that work for us? Talk to your colleagues about the examples. Look out for your own examples. Try to understand your business through the

Hallmarks that we have identified. For example, how effective is your networking?

Try not to simply read the examples passively but fit them into your world. In this way you will start to develop your business.

Level 2: Assessment

The purpose of the assessment sections is to encourage you to assess and learn more about your own business and its potential. It provides a process to enable you to complete all the assessment sections summarized at the end of this book (Toolkit 1).

One of the difficulties in assessing your own business is that you are often too close to it and can't see the wood for the trees. If you are to develop your business you need an objective assessment of current reality: facts not opinions, specifics not generalities, solid information not myths or fantasy.

In order to gather factual information, assessments help you with some key questions. Try to answer them as honestly as possible, there is no point doing a PR job on yourself!

There are two major sources of information to enable you to assess your business objectively:

Internal: *Management colleagues and staff.*
External: *Customers.*

Internal When completing the assessment sections it will help if you ask people inside your business to answer the questions. Assemble your top team and put the questions to them to answer. Ask your network for their views. Try to be open-minded, for you may not like all the answers you get. If all you want to hear is that you are wonderful then perhaps you should not undertake the exercise. Most businesses have strengths and weaknesses, and you and your business will undoubtedly be the same. The purpose of asking other people is to enable you to identify your own particular blind spots.

To help you obtain some objective feedback internally the assessment sections of the book have been compiled into a questionnaire (Toolkit 1). Photocopy this section and ask your people to complete it, and also complete it yourself. You can then assess and compare your ratings with those of your staff. You are strongly recommended to take this step. For example:

- *Do your scores differ from your fellow directors?*
- *Are there different scores at different levels in the business?*
- *Which Hallmarks are strengths (high scores) and which are weaknesses (low scores).*

This information is vital if you are going to take positive action to develop your business.

Remember that, internally, people will tell you (if you are the boss) what they think you want to hear. Good news upwards is normal, and you often need to dig deeper to get closer to the truth, to what people really think.

Make a note of the responses you get. If you ask enough people and dig deeply enough you will get a clear picture of the reality of your business. You can then move forward and develop.

External   All businesses say they know and understand their customers: 'We deal with them every day.' This presents a problem in gathering objective information. A businessman said to me recently when questioned about the quality of their Customerising, 'We must be OK – we don't get many complaints.' Frankly, if your customer service perception is based on complaints then sell the business today! Very often we are so close that we cannot see the real picture. It can be helpful to stand back and undertake a systematic review of customers' perception of your business.

The way to do this is to complete a customer perception survey. Exactly how this should be done is laid out step by step as Toolkit 2. This information will enable you to assess your business objectively and develop it successfully. Again, you are strongly recommended to take this step, for the basis of competitive advantage is better information on customers.

Level 3: Action

Action brings either success or learning. Successful companies get into action quickly and do not suffer paralysis by analysis. This section seeks to encourage you to try things out, experiment, have a go. It includes tips and ideas in order to develop your business. It also includes step-by-step actions to take to encourage you to have a go and ask the question, 'How will this benefit my business?'. Learning takes place when options are increased. This book aims to increase your options. Here are some things that good learners do:

- *Take risks – they have a go, try new ideas.*
- *Are prepared to be wrong – no one can be right all the time. If we are to learn then we need to let go of the past and admit we were wrong.*
- *Ask questions – learners are always asking questions. Why did that happen? How does it work? How can we improve?*
- *Tolerate ambiguity – there are no 'right' answers in business. If there were we would all be multimillionaires! Learners recognize that business is about opportunities and percentages.*
- *Do not take themselves too seriously – business is serious but it can be fun, and when it is fun we seem to make progress.*
- *Are optimistic – optimism rubs off on others, and builds energy and commitment.*

Conversely, non-learners also seem to do certain things:

- *Stay quiet – they never take risks, never get involved. They may be cynical and quietly arrogant.*
- *Want definitive answers – non-learners want the magic key.*

- *Rationalize – Yes, but ... It won't work here because ... We tried it once ... Our business is different ...*
- *Quote past precedents (normally out of context) – We tried that twenty years ago and ... , I selected Fred and he's a star. (They forget to tell you about the other twenty they 'selected' who have since been sacked.)*
- *Are pessimistic – The recession ... The Japanese ... It won't work ... There's no point trying ...*

Learners, then, are open-minded, while non-learners have closed minds, but one thing is clear: no one can teach you anything unless you decide that you want to learn.

Accelerated Learning

There is no doubt that the school of experience is the best teacher. However, the tuition fees can be expensive! It also can take time to learn and develop. It is, nevertheless, possible to accelerate your learning process. It requires doing things consciously rather than unconsciously by adding a couple of steps into your normal way of operating. Once you are comfortable with the approach you begin to operate it unconsciously.

Normal operating method   Accelerated learning process

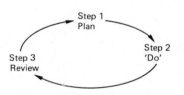

Step 1: Plan

1. *Consider the assessments in this book. Which aspects of your business would benefit from some new ideas or a new approach?*

25

2. *Where do you score low on the assessments? What should you focus upon to gain maximum benefit to your business right now?*
3. *What impacts on customers? What parts of your business do you want to improve? Select an area to work upon.*

Whenever you choose to tackle something in a different way it can be stressful. This is because you are out of your 'comfort zone'. Comfort zones are the tried and tested, the familiar, the predictable.

Example: *When you visit your favourite restaurant and sit at your familiar table and eat your favourite food you feel good. Whenever you try a restaurant for the first time, especially with friends, you can feel slightly anxious and concerned. What will it be like? If you are not careful you look for things to confirm your worst fears, particularly if it wasn't your idea in the first place! You need to be optimistically realistic, otherwise, 'I know it will be awful' (a prediction) turns into reality – 'See, I knew we shouldn't have tried something different.'*

Here are some practical tips for planning to do something different:

1. *Start with something important.*
2. *Focus on the benefit of the improvement. Do not dwell on what might go wrong, but anticipate it as a success. Focus on success, not failure, in your mind.*
3. *Work on it in an incremental way, one step at a time. Break the issues down into logical steps, steps that are not too large for you to tackle comfortably.*

Step 2: Do

Little scope for theory here. Go for it!

Step 3: Review

Too often the review gets missed out, with the danger that we repeat the same mistakes. One businessman told me he had twenty years' experience of selling. It turned out that he had one year's experience twenty times, because he made the same mistakes over and over again: he never reviewed his performance.

Adding review to your normal way of operating has major benefits, not only to your learning but to your business development. Do it consciously until it becomes automatic. Here is how:

Consider the Accelerated Learning Review Process form on page 29, which may be photocopied. Think of a recent incident in your business, and fill in the form. You will probably find that treating the experience as a conscious process helped you to learn.

If you keep trying new ideas and reviewing your performance your learning is greatly accelerated and your business can develop so far it can get ahead of the competition.

The Japanese have a word for what we have described: they call it *kaizen*. They also ascribe much of their success to the process of constant improvement. Think of the power that could be unleashed in your business if everybody took this approach!

Here is an example from our research companies:

Step 1: Plan

Area to improve from customer perception survey: Delivery on time.
Company rating (out of 10): 5. Competition rating (out of 10): 8.
Delivery was rated second in priority by customers, and a major competitor is perceived as having a significant advantage over this company. The benefits of matching or leading the competitor on delivery were considered highly significant to the business in competitive terms.

They mapped out a simple plan:

1. *Put in a simple recording system to establish current delivery performance.*
2. *Assess current performance over a two-week period.*
3. *Set a target of 80 per cent delivery on time within three months.*
4. *Monitor and feed back the results at the weekly management meeting using the 'review' process format.*
5. *The managing director to take personal control of the project.*

Step 2: Do

They put in a simple recording system and after two weeks had enough data to analyse.

Step 3: Review

1. *What went well:*
   The dispatcher filled in delivery forms accurately.
   The drivers began to talk about 'delivery performance' and take it seriously.
2. *What went badly:*
   The forms were not filled in when the dispatcher was on holiday for two days.
   The system was not explained to the production team, so they obstructed it.
   In general, people did not know why the system was put in.
3. *As a result of steps 1 and 2, what would you do differently?*
   (i)
   (ii)
   (iii)
   (iv)
   (v) .

The company then progressed to Step 3 of the review and carried out the improvements.

Accelerated Learning
Review Process

Step 1   List all the things that went well:

Step 2   List all the things that went badly:

Step 3   As a result of Steps 1 and 2, what will you do differently next time?

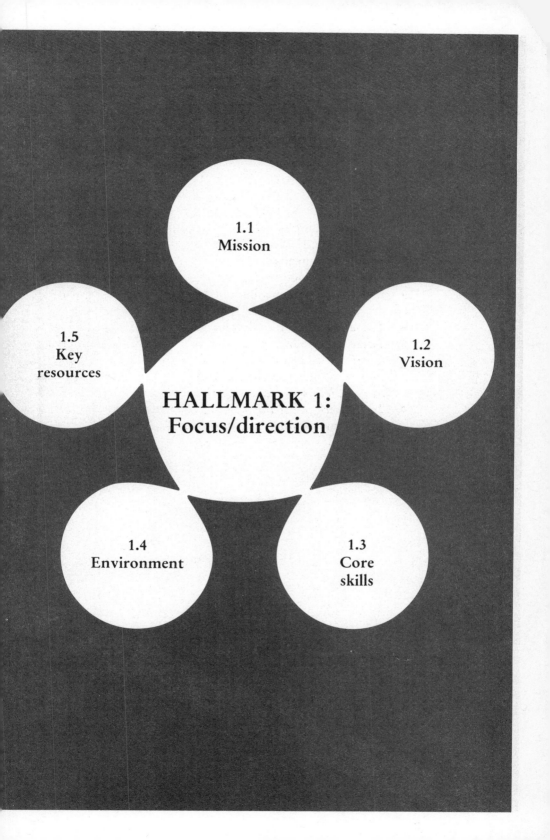

Successful companies share many common features, although each one creates its own recipe for success. One common feature is clear focus and direction. This enables people to harness their personal energies and to add value to the business. This section outlines the key principles involved in the process of fashioning and managing overall focus and direction.

The key here is to think long term around the Hallmark and then to ensure that each factor on the Hallmark supports the others. For example, what key resources do we require to deliver the vision? How can we use our core skills to satisfy our customers' needs?

The same principles apply as those outlined with the original Business Development Framework. But remember:

- *These are principles, not magic formulae.*
- *These principles are sequential. Start with mission and work clockwise around the Hallmark. You will find that there is a logical sequence from 1 to 5, and that you need to complete one stage before moving on to the next.*
- *In practice, most businesses work with several principles at one time – they are interdependent.*

1.1
Mission

Awareness / What business are we in?

One of the apparently easiest yet in practice most difficult business questions to answer is, What business are we *really* in? This has been called the mission of the business.

Here are some examples of mission:

AbleClean:	*Quality cleaning for the North-east*
Derwent Valley Foods:	*Quality adult snackfoods*
Darfen:	*Security systems*
Neat Ideas:	*Mail-order office products*

The purpose of missions is to draw a boundary round the scope of the business: to define the business clearly and communicate it to people so they can use it as a framework for decision-making and to add value. These missions differ from the classical statements normally associated with large companies in that they are shorter and do not attempt to be all-encompassing. They serve to describe the business in a simple way. Here are some guidelines.

1. *A powerful mission statement is short, clear and simple. It has between six and ten words. It rolls off people's tongues.*
2. *It states clearly what business you are in.*
3. *It avoids generalities.*
4. *It focuses on what the organization is now rather than what it might be in the future.*

Developing a mission provides a good illustration of how the Hallmarks work in practice. In order to determine what business you are in you need to consider what are you good at (core skills) and what opportunities exist for you (environment). You need to work around the Hallmark in order to craft an effective mission. This highlights the interdependence of the principles in the Hallmark model.

In our success companies we noted that:

1. *They had a mission that was communicated from the top.*
2. *Management actions reinforced the mission. The decisions they took, the questions they asked, the issue or agendas.*
3. *People do not argue about the mission – only how they can add value to it.*
4. *The best missions also motivate people. They want to contribute to a greater good.*

So what is your mission?

It is difficult for outsiders to see what inspires employees in a mission. Take DHPs, for example. 'Developing people and organizations' appears bland, until you know that this applies to employees just as much as it does to customers. Every employee has a personal development plan, which they find very motivating. This reinforces the key issue on mission. It needs to be more than just words. You need to demonstrate your commitment to it and build trust through your people.

1.1 Mission

Assessment

Tick here if this is true for your business

1. We have a clearly articulated mission that fits the criteria for mission established in this Section.   [ ]

2. We use our mission to provide focus for our business decisions.   [ ]

3. Our mission describes accurately our true identity and what we are about.   [ ]

4. Everyone in our business understands our mission. [ ]

5. Our people behave in line with the spirit of the mission.   [ ]

6. Our people find it easy to contribute to our mission.   [ ]

If you can honestly tick all six questions you have a clear mission that is driving your business. You might want to move on to other parts of out Framework. Fewer than four ticks and you might decide to improve your Focus/Direction by moving on to the next section, *Action*. This aims to help you take action to improve your business, to translate knowledge into a profitable improvement to your business.

1.1 Mission

Action   Select any action you want to take to develop your business. This might be as a result of the assessment, feedback from your people, or preferably your customer perception survey.

Action 1:   If you already have a mission statement ask yourself these key questions and take action on the answers:

- *Does it meet the criteria set out in our Awareness section?*
- *Who knows about it?*
- *Do we really use it to make decisions?*
- *Do we need to shape it up?*

Action 2:   If you do not have a mission then consider developing one. Answer the question what business are we really in, by:

A   *Looking historically at where you have made money on projects, products or services.*

B   *Assessing opportunities in your environment. What opportunities exist for your business?*

Combine the answers to the questions in A and B together to make C – your mission.

This is the essence of strategic thinking – the process of synthesis (bringing together) as opposed to analysis, which is breaking down into parts.

Action 3:   Publish your mission.

- *Put it on the back of your business cards.*
- *Put it upon a sign in reception.*
- *Add it to your letterheads and stationery.*
- *Talk about it to your people.*

Action 4:   Try to think strategically about your mission and encourage your people to do the same. People think at three different levels:

1 Tactical: Fixing problems, e.g. how to deal with customer complaints.
2 Operational: How can I improve our admin systems?
3 Strategic: Our strategy calls for growth so how can I rethink how we do business in order to get an immediate 25 per cent increase? This involves transformational thinking.

To encourage yourself and your managers to think strategically discuss the three levels of thinking which will add value to your mission.

Our mission (strategy) calls for

. . . .

Therefore we will

. . . .
. . . .
. . . .

**1.2
Vision**

Awareness / Spelling out the future you want

Vision is about having some idea of the kind of future we want and committing ourselves to getting there. This may not be simply in terms of making a million pounds in five years – vision is often much broader. In fact, not one of our success companies set out to make a million!

The problem for most of us is that the simple question, 'What do we really want?' is very difficult to answer. Goal clarification is a lifelong process. It is about growing up and maturing. In the process of clarifying your goals, try to stop worrying about how you will get there. If the goals are important enough, you will invent ways to achieve them. One company chairman told us, 'We can't predict the future in our industry, so we don't try. We just invent it.'

If we then consider our present business and are dissatisfied we move towards the new vision. You were encouraged to complete a Customer Perception Survey earlier in this book. Hopefully, it triggered some actions to improve and move towards the picture you have of your business, how you would like it to be.

Vision creates new standards for your future. It could include:

- *Where will we be positioned in the industry/market?*
- *Who will we be doing business with?*
- *What will be happening then that is not happening now?*
- *What lifestyle will I have?*

Vision is about creating a clear picture of the future you want to create for yourself and your business, then working out goals for your business.

The next stage is to communicate that vision to energize and motivate the people to want to be part of your vision. The key job of any leader is to create a vision and sell it to people. You are a powerful role model whether you like it or not.

> **Example:** *One of my customers was considering developing a new vision with the management team. However, the consensus of the team was that they were not ready for it because the chief executive was focused in history – last month's accounts. All his questions were about the past. All his concerns seemed to be about how they did last month. There was never any discussion about the future. The message to the team was to forget the future, yesterday is what matters. He presented the wrong message to his people.*

Vision is about stretching out and taking a big leap. It is not about business planning, the definition of which in many businesses seems to be last year's sales plus 10 per cent plus hope!

A key message in this book is that the limiting factor on growth of your business is not funds, time, people, the government, interest rates, or the next-door neighbour's dog – the limiting factor is your vision! If your vision is powerful enough and people are committed to it, *you will invent the way.* You will solve problems, find resources, make contacts, obtain finance, and get there. So how far out can your vision be?

Remember, it is up to you. It is fine to have a vision that is last year's sales plus 10 per cent if that is what you *really* want. We are not all the same. Some want to conquer the world, others want to reduce their golf handicap to 10.

So, I hear you ask, what is your vision, Hall? Come on, own up, you don't have one, do you?

In 1982, when I started in business, it was to survive for twelve months! In 1985 it became to have my own business in the North of England. In 1988 it was to be in the top twenty consultancy firms in the UK. In 1990 it became to operate in Europe, the USA, and Australia, to become a world leader in strategy and business development. We have achieved the first three visions and are still working on the fourth.

To be successful we need two things:

1. *Clearly state what future we want – **vision**.*
2. *Get our team behind us in moving towards our vision – **teamwork**.*

Our vision is to become a world leader in business strategy and development. Now, I don't know how I am going to achieve this latest vision, but the point is that at this stage I don't have to. All I need is the belief I can do it, and I may well succeed. This is fundamental because it creates the energy, the driving force. It is about faith, belief without evidence. There can be no facts about the future, only belief.

This personal illustration indicates another key point. When we arrive at our destination, our energy shuts down. We become blasé and complacent, bored with success. Therefore we need to renew our vision, otherwise we just disappear. A key job of the top management of any business is to create the future vision and communicate it to people. Once we get a critical mass of people behind us, then anything is possible. That's your job.

Example: *My employer was not doing his customers any favours; it was all done on the cheap. I decided to do it and supply the quality the customer was after. I wanted to bring real quality into the cleaning business. My vision was all about quality. It worked, and we doubled the price. Superior Cleaning Specialists*

Example: *Panda Supplies holds joint meetings with customers, suppliers and staff to keep them updated on the company's progress. They make it fun and enjoyable so people want to attend.*

1.2 Vision

Assessment

*Tick if this is
true for your
business*

1. *We have a clear vision for our future.*   [   ]

2. *We communicate our vision to our people at every possible opportunity.*   [   ]

3. *Our vision energizes and provides an incentive for everyone in our business.*   [   ]

4. *We seem to find ways of moving towards our vision.*   [   ]

5. *Our vision changes as our dreams become reality.* [   ]

6. *We are future-focused rather than being trapped by history (or how things used to be).*   [   ]

Fewer than four ticks and you need to take *Action*.

1.2 Vision

Action   **Action 1:**   When you have time, take your team away for a day or two. Talk about the future you want to create. Craft a vision for the future, and involve your team in the process. Here is how to do it.

Step 1:   Put these questions to your team: in three years

- Who do we really want to do business with?
- How should we treat our people?
- What style do we want to have?
- Where will we be positioned in the industry?

Step 2:   Get them to write down answers to these questions.

Step 3:   Discuss each other's answers. Debate them until you get common agreement and commitment to your future.

Step 4:   Publish the results for everyone to see.

Action 2:   Take every opportunity to discuss your vision with your people. Don't assume they know or have thought about it. That's your job. Once they have clear direction they will search for ways to make it happen. Five hundred people focused on achieving your visions have to be better than one.

Action 3:   Talk to suppliers, customers, your network, about your vision. They will help you. You will be amazed.

Action 4: Create a vision that seems too big – for example, expansion to the USA. Small visions do not motivate anybody.

Awareness / What are you fundamentally good at

> **Example:** *Keepmoat, which operates in the construction industry, analysed which type of work historically had been profitable for them. Over 20 years they consistently made money on refurbishment contracts (smartening up council houses), building new houses and design build contracts. They either made or lost money on their other activities but in an unpredictable way. They decided to stick to the three areas of core skill. In five years they quadrupled their sales and profits. They became the twelfth best performing UK business out of 10,000 in a national survey, coming from nowhere. Yet the middle managers wanted to employ their creativity by taking on more 'exciting projects' (exciting for whom?). They were bored with making lots of money.*

This example illustrates some of the key issues when focusing on core skills.

- *Work out carefully what you are good at. This may be narrower than you think. In our example they were consistently successful in only three core skill areas.*
- *Core skills are developed over time normally as a result of a lot of problem-solving (learning) – accumulated 'know-how'.*
- *Core skills are product or process development on the job – skills are developed with customers. They are usually crafted from experience.*

The example also highlights an interesting paradox of focusing on core skills. Often the things that make us money are those we also find boring. We want to create some excitement in our lives, so we diversify and become completely unstuck. Tom Peters tells companies to 'stick to the knitting' – do what you are good at. This seems to fit with our successful companies' experiences. Ace Conveyors, for example, have considerable engineering expertise yet they focus on supplying and maintaining conveyors because that is what they are good at – 'our core skills are in conveyors'.

I learned two more important lessons from our companies. Not only do companies get bored with their core product/service skills, they can also grow bored with their business-generating methods. The top management may get business, say, by visiting customers or attending trade fairs. They get fed up with this mode, neglect it, and sales drop. They then panic and throw money at an advertising campaign – the wrong promotional channel. It fails. Successful companies 'stick to the knitting' not only in products but also with their primary business-gathering method. If it works, don't knock it!

Core skills are those which are defined by your customers and not you. This is a crucial point. One consultancy company thought their competitive advantage was the quality of the reports they produced. However, a survey revealed that their customers perceived the quality of their reports to be similar to that of their competitors – they had no real competitive advantage. However, customers did perceive that they had a competitive advantage through the quality of the relationships they established with them. Once the consultancy firm was aware of this competitive advantage they could try to leverage it into developing new business. So competitive advantage can be seen as a set of core skills unique to a business.

Example: *When we were first set up we made any-thing and everything, we were fighting for business, and anything that was plastic we tried. Then we looked at what we were good at and what the market really wanted and decided to focus on lipstick con-tainers and compacts. Now 60 per cent of our busi-ness is in lipstick containers, 40 per cent in compacts. We took off when we decided to focus on what we were good at. Cresstale*

1.3 Core Skills

Assessment

*Tick here if this
is true for your
business*

1. Our core skills are clearly defined, and we stick
    to them at all times.   [ ]
2. We are constantly trying to nourish and expand
    our core skills.   [ ]
3. Our customers confirm our own view of our core
    skills.   [ ]
4. We are good at developing our core skills into new
    opportunities.   [ ]
5. Our core skills provide us with competitive
    advantage with our customers.   [ ]
6. Our core skills fit clearly with our vision for our
    future.   [ ]

Fewer than four ticks and you need to take *Action*.

1.3 Core Skills

Action

Action 1: Assess historically where you make money: which products, projects, or services? Stick to these in the future.

Action 2: Assess how you get business effectively: is it face to face, exhibitions, mailshots? Stick to the proven method in the future.

Action 3: Decide how you can leverage or utilize your core skills and build your business. One training organization's core skill was speaking skills in front of groups on training programmes. Having confirmed this as a core skill they decided to use it to build their business by attending and speaking at conferences which trainers attended, in order to sell their services. They doubled their size in six months!

Action 4: Update your core skills on an on-going basis. Do not expect your competitors to play fair and not try to chip away at your advantages. You need to keep your skills up to date and ahead of your competitors.

Here are some ideas to help you achieve this aim:

- *Who are the best in the business? What do they do? (This is called benchmarking.)*
- *Your upgrading of core skills will inevitably at some point include the use of IT. Discuss with an IT specialist how you can develop your business.*
- *Challenge your people. Make it an adventure. Put it on the agenda. How can we develop our core skills?*

- *Read 'Kaizan': The Key to Japan's Competitive Success*, Masaaki Imai, published by McGraw-Hill Publishing Co, Maidenhead, 1989.

Awareness / Scanning the environment for threats and opportunities

Our successful companies had business plans with clearly defined missions, visions and objectives. This did not stop them from acting opportunistically. Growth appears to come as a result of getting organized to identify and take opportunities. Growth is seen as a series of projects (opportunities) rather than a grand scheme or detailed blue-print. These findings are in line with much of the research into growth companies conducted by Durham University Business School.

Scanning the environment for opportunities and threats involves three steps:

1. *Developing a 'culture of vigilance' to identify threats and opportunities.*
2. *Analysing the information gathered.*
3. *Developing projects to take up opportunities or guard against threats.*

In order to scan the environment successful companies stay close to the action and network with people. This provides information about threats and opportunities. An environmental map may assist the process. This can help you see the world more clearly and get rid of some blind spots. Such a map consists of questions to ask in key areas:

- *What is the government going to do that might affect our business?*
- *How will the changes in the economy affect us?*

- *What are the industry trends?*
- *What are our competitors up to?*

Each company needs to develop its own map in order to track the environment for opportunities and threats. Here is a simple map for my business.

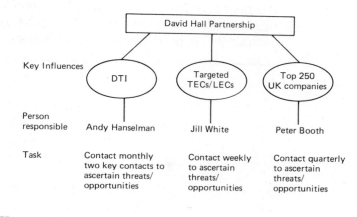

	David Hall Partnership	
Key Influences	DTI — Targeted TECs/LECs — Top 250 UK companies	
Person responsible	Andy Hanselman — Jill White — Peter Booth	
Task	Contact monthly two key contacts to ascertain threats/ opportunities — Contact weekly to ascertain threats/ opportunities — Contact quarterly to ascertain threats/ opportunities	

Key questions:
- *What's happening?*
- *What future plans do you have?*
- *How do you see the future?*
- *What are the key issues for next year?*

Key factors can be ascertained by again using questions specific to your business. One of our research companies was thinking of opening a restaurant as an opportunity. They asked:

- *What is the failure rate for restaurants in this area?*
- *Why do they die?*
- *Who are our potential customers?*
- *How will a VAT increase affect the business?*
- *What do our competitors offer?*
- *How long will it take us to get established?*
- *How has unemployment affected eating habits in the area?*

Information can then be gathered to assess the opportunity. Once an opportunity has been assessed then plans can be laid to exploit it. Do you know what is really happening in your business environment?

> **Example:** *I can make three telephone calls to find out exactly what is happening in our business environment. These people keep their ear to the ground and are paid to monitor trends. We get instant feedback on opportunities and threats. We could not operate without this information. A research company*

Assessment

Tick here if this
is true for your
business

1. We are very effective at scanning our business
    environment.   [ ]

2. We are constantly identifying threats and oppor-
    tunities to our business.   [ ]

3. We have created more opportunities than we can
    handle.   [ ]

4. We have effective intelligence-gathering systems.   [ ]

5. We are rarely taken by surprise by our business
    environment.   [ ]

6. We feel we manage rather than are being managed
    by our environment.   [ ]

Fewer than four ticks and you need to take *Action*.

1.4 Environment

Action   **Action 1:**   Create an environment map to assist you in the process of monitoring your environment.

Step 1:   Use the checklist to identify those areas that affect your business.

- *Customer needs* [ ]
- *Government policy* [ ]
- *Government agencies* [ ]
- *Economy* [ ]
- *Political climate* [ ]
- *Competitors* [ ]
- *Changing demographics* [ ]
- *Industry trends* [ ]
- *Technology* [ ]
- *International events* [ ]
- *Social trends* [ ]
- [ ]
- [ ]
- [ ]

Include your own factors.

Step 2:   Use the map frequently to scan your business environment for threats and opportunities.

Step 3:   Report the key issues at management meetings.

55

Action 2:	Ask your trade body for reports on the business environment.
Action 3:	Obtain a DTI Enterprise Grant for researching your business environment.
Action 4:	Stay close to your main contacts. Develop a 'culture of vigilance' towards your business contacts.
Action 5:	Talk to anybody who can be helpful to your business.
Action 6:	Attend as many free business presentations in your area in the evenings as you can. Talk to people.

Awareness / Identify and maintain a supply of key resources

Some resources are essential if your business is to succeed. Some key resources may be readily available, while others may need organizing. Key resources are those that enable you to do business effectively. These may include:

–	Money:	Access to capital and funds for growth.
–	Materials:	Basic raw materials may require planning and managing, particularly if they are in short supply.
–	People:	Lack of people resources is often the limiting factor in the development of a successful business.
–	Technology:	Do you have the right technology to compete?
–	Brainpower:	Do you have creative ideas or problem-solving abilities?
–	Information:	A critical resource today.
–	Contacts/Network:	Contacts are a key resource in the development of any business.
–	Customer base:	Is it large enough and well defined?
–	Image:	Can create business for you if it is positive.

The availability of herbs and spices that grow in certain climates is a key resource for Derwent Valley Foods. Vehicles are essential to enable Superior Cleaning Specialists to do their work in cleaning telephone boxes. They are a key resource: funding was a problem, sixteen banks said 'no' to lending the necessary money but the seventeenth agreed. The distribution network is a key resource for Neat Ideas, enabling them to achieve a 90 per cent customer service level on delivery – on time.

Key resources control your move towards your vision.

> Our key resources are our contacts in Eastern Europe. We know who to talk with to develop our business. Without these resources we could not operate effectively and certainly could not develop our business. Chameleon Design

Developing businesses often need access to capital. They also need effective people to drive the business forward. Access to information can be a critical resource. If I understand my customers' real needs better than my competitors do I can exploit this opportunity.

In summary, key resources support vision, but then, so does every other principle in this Hallmark. Focus and Direction come from thinking through these long-term issues and ensuring that all the principles support each other in an integrated way.

1.5 Key Resources

Assessment

1. *We have identified and ensured that we have a regular supply of key resources.* [ ]

2. *Our key resources support the focus and direction of our business.* [ ]

3. *Our business will not be stifled by the lack of key resources in the future.* [ ]

4. *We have made plans to ensure a continuous supply of key resources.* [ ]

5. *Our people resource is well managed and adds real value to our business.* [ ]

Fewer than four ticks and you need to take *Action*.

1.5 Key Resources

Action   Action 1:   Identify the key resources required to achieve your objectives.

Step 1:   List your vision and customer needs.
Step 2:   Assess key resources required to meet Step 1 using the following checklist:

	Tick those important to your business	*Tick those of which you have an effective supply*
	A	B
• *People*	[ ]	[ ]
• *Materials*	[ ]	[ ]
• *Energy*	[ ]	[ ]
• *Information*	[ ]	[ ]
• *Technology*	[ ]	[ ]
• *Capital*	[ ]	[ ]
• *Natural resources*	[ ]	[ ]
• *Contacts*	[ ]	[ ]
• *Partners*	[ ]	[ ]
• *Company image*	[ ]	[ ]
• *Others*	[ ]	[ ]

Step 3:   Assess your current resources and plan your future supply by considering the gaps between A and B.

Action 2:   Get an independent person or body to assess the quality of your key resources – for example, obtain government funding and TEC-backed initiatives such as Business Growth Training Option 3 (a grant scheme to assist growth companies to train and develop their staff).

Action 3:   Consider your people resources. Are they good enough to deliver your vision? What development do they need? Talk to your local TEC about development programmes such as Investors in People.

2.1
Developing
a customer
commitment

2.5
Market
development

2.2
Networking

HALLMARK 2:
Customerising

2.4
Customer
delight

2.3
Problem
seeking
Problem
solving

Total customer commitment = customerising. This chapter shows you how to systematically customerise the business through awareness, assessment and action. Customerising is a distillation from our research of the way successful companies stay close to customers, seek and solve their problems to create customer delight.

The process of customerising focuses resources on to customer contact on an ongoing basis. Some people have called this relationship marketing. Success companies seek out important customers and spend considerable time with them, helping them solve real problems. They develop skills in a specific area, sharpening and shaping those skills over time. They go out of their way to delight customers by providing that bit extra. Hence customerising.

Awareness / Every action taken considers the impact on customers

How can you develop customer commitment? What experiences shape this commitment?

In the case of Superior Cleaning Specialists the owner had previously worked for British Telecom and was dissatisfied with the quality of cleaning services provided. He decided to set up in business 'to do it better', supplying cleaning services to British Telecom. He developed his customer commitment from the experiences of being on the receiving end – the school of experience.

Derwent Valley Foods management team worked in the snack food business. They spotted opportunities to serve customers better so they set up their own operation.

In other cases customer commitment is developed by staying close to customers, listening and responding to their needs. Ace Conveyors' 24-hour customer service policy evolved from solving customer problems. Problem-solving is learning.

In every case the key people set the standard and created the examples for others in their company to follow. One owner-manager put it well: 'In every decision we ask the question, what value will this add to our customers' business? If our answer is positive we do it. Everybody in our business recognizes it is not the geniuses in the boardroom who pay the wages, it's our customers.'

This attitude should be the norm, but unfortunately in my experience it is the exception. In Metro FM's car park, spaces for customers are conveniently near to reception. In many businesses the convenient parking spaces are reserved for directors.

These are simple examples, but they indicate clearly an attitude of mind towards customers. It is the little things that count.

> **Example:** *I visited one of the researched companies for the first time. The security guard at the gate knew my name and asked me to park next to Reception. The receptionist greeted me by name (how?) and asked me to take a seat while she filled in the visitors' book on my behalf. Ten seconds after I was seated a lady appeared with a black coffee in a nice china cup. (How did she know that is what I wanted without asking?) My contact's PA arrived and informed me she would be with me in two and a half minutes. At the stroke of 10.30 she emerged, greeted me very warmly, and escorted me to her office. I didn't need to see their accounts to know they were successful. . . .*
>
> *I visited another of our researched companies the following day. The security guard wandered over, sighing deeply, and informed me that there was a public car park approximately half a mile away. Eventually I arrived at reception. I was requested to fill in a book. The receptionist sniffed at me, looked me up and down (he obviously thought I was selling double glazing) and told me to wait. I found a coffee machine with paper cups. After having been kept waiting twenty minutes I was ushered into a small meeting room. I didn't need to see their accounts either. . . .*
> *Dinah Bennett, DUBS*

How do you get customer commitment? It starts at the top. It is your job to set the example. You cannot delegate the responsibility.

Example: *A young man who could not read or write joined our business start-up programme at Chesterfield. He wanted to start a roof-tiling business. He placed a small advertisement in the local paper. He installed a telephone answering machine at home and went about his business. When he arrived home and before sitting down to dinner he played all his messages back and rang potential customers. He then visited them immediately and gave them a quote. Only then did he return home for dinner. He understood the need to respond quickly to customers and as a result has a full order book.*

2.1 Developing Customer Commitment

Assessment Using the information gathered internally and externally, answer the questions as objectively as you can.

*Tick here if this
is true for your
business*

1. *Customers find it easy to buy from us.*   [ ]

2. *We do not employ any 'sales prevention' officers here.*   [ ]

3. *Top management sets high standards and provides good examples of our customer commitment.*   [ ]

4. *We are committed to understanding the differences between our customers' needs and wants.*   [ ]

5. *We can provide six good examples of our commitment to customers from our last month's activity.*   [ ]

6. *Customer commitment is a way of life in our business.*   [ ]

Fewer than four ticks and you might decide to improve your Customerising by moving on to the next section, *Action*.

2.1 Developing customer commitment

Action   This is the *action* sequence.

Action 1:   If you haven't done so already, conduct a detailed customer perception survey along the lines suggested in Toolkit 2 in order to assess your current level of customer commitment.

Action 2:   Take any aspect of your business (preferably one that has been identified by your customer perception survey) and improve it. Set yourself an objective to achieve this month, such as:

- *Double deliveries on time, eg 40% to 80%.*
- *Get quotations back in forty-eight hours rather than a week.*
- *Contact all key customers at least once by telephone this month.*

Action 3:   Ask your key customers this question over the next month: 'How easy are we to buy from?' Act on the results.

Action 4:   Set one example of customer commitment that is highly visible this week, for example:

- *Personally deliver or return an important quotation by hand the same day.*
- *Put a system in place to record how customers who visit take their refreshments. Make it an automatic process to surprise them.*

Action 5:	Visit a key customer to learn more about their business rather than sell them your product.
Action 6:	Invite a customer to visit your premises to learn more about your business.
Action 7:	Occasionally hand-write a short personal note on letters to your customers.
Action 8:	Consider whether to hand out service comments card to gauge customer reactions.
Action 9:	Give customers your home or portable telephone number.
Action 10:	Pass on copies of articles and information intelligence to customers.
Action 11:	Place a 'customer welcome' board in reception.

**Awareness / Actively working with those who can influence
your business**

There are many people who can influence the performance of
your business. The obvious ones are customers, suppliers,
employees, and banks. However, there are also less obvious
influences. For example, signposters. These are people who
can signpost opportunities, contacts, or customers in the
direction of your business.

> **Example:** *We wondered why we did not get any
> enquiries fed to us by a particular Enterprise Agency.
> The director assured us that we should be getting
> prospects offered. A detailed review revealed that the
> receptionist, who referred all enquiries to consultants,
> did not have us on her list. It was a simple clerical
> error, costing us a potential £100,000 in sales per
> year!*

How effective are your signposters? Check them out.

A second set of network contacts that are less visible but
very important are the key influences. To understand their
part in your business requires an introduction to the idea of
networking.

Networking is simply developing and maintaining relationships with the people who can affect and impact directly
or indirectly on your business. It gives you access to
contacts, information, leads, threats, opportunities, ideas,

role models, and many other benefits. Think of it like a spider's web:

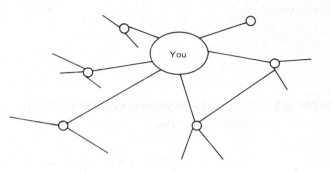

The spider's web consists of you at the centre of your key contacts. These contacts are also connected to others. By cultivating certain contacts you can have access to many of the elements that affect your business. The key influencers are those people at the intersections of the spider's web, the people you contact if you want to know what is really happening in one area.

Ace Conveyors contacted one person at British Coal to find out what was happening in the coal business in Yorkshire. The point about the key influences are that they require nurturing and attention. Who are the key influences on your network and are they active on your behalf?

Everybody has a network. Your job is to energize it. This means building relationships and being active with the key players. Two factors clearly emerged from our research. First, top management talk regularly to their network contacts. They had their home telephone numbers and contacted them on a daily or weekly basis. Networkers had immediate access to top management at all times – and they used it.

Secondly, key players travel. Typically our successful managers travel 40,000 miles annually visiting customers, suppliers and their network contacts. 'We make the foods on Monday and we are on the road Tuesday, Wednesday, Thursday, and Friday networking,' say Derwent Valley Foods.

Networking involves regular contact with a purpose. This can be exchanging useful information, passing on news, and doing favours. One company described the process as: 'Think of how you treat your best friends and do the same with your network.'

One caution – some established networks may not be appropriate for your business. One company related a tale where the chairman spent all his time 'networking' at Round Table and Chamber of Commerce lunches and The Lions and Institute of Directors dinners. He got fat, but the business didn't! He got it wrong simply because none of the people who attended these functions were really part of his network (that is, could directly influence his business). Focus on networks that contribute towards your vision. These may not be the ones you necessarily enjoy most.

A final issue from my own business experience. Sometimes we build a strong relationship with one person as a key customer, who provides us with lots of opportunities. Then they leave and everything stops. The need is to build a network inside the customer's organization so that we are not dependent on one person. Yes, I know it's obvious but we fell for it and so will you.

Are you dependent on one good relationship in a key customer?

Example: *We contacted the Northern Development Corporation to find out which companies are entering our area and we make contact with them. We go in at the highest possible level as we did with a Japanese company recently. We were in dialogue with them long before they moved here. When they did set up, they knew us well. Panda Supplies*

Assessment

1. *We understand our network and how it impacts upon our business.*   [   ]

2. *Networking is a top management responsibility in our business.*   [   ]

3. *Top management spend enough time networking with key customers.*   [   ]

4. *We are not dependent on individual contact with key customers; we have many contacts.*   [   ]

5. *Networking creates more new opportunities than we can cope with.*   [   ]

6. *Networking is discussed and planned for frequently at our management meetings.*   [   ]

Fewer than four ticks and you need to take *Action*.

2.2 Networking

Action Action 1: **Manage your network.**

Step 1: List your key network contacts by constructing a diagram as follows:

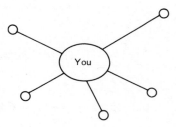

Step 2: Mark the names as follows:

+ If they act positively for your business.
− If they have a negative impact on your business.
= If they are neutral.

Step 3: Make a plan to use the + to build your business. How can you convert the − to +? How will you encourage the = to get off the fence and act positively?

Tick those names you consider you contact frequently enough and use an X to indicate those you need to contact more frequently. Transfer these decisions into your diary or time planner.

Action 2: Use your existing network to build up others who could be of assistance to your business. Use their network to build up yours. (Eighty per cent of our new business in 1990 came from this action alone.) It works. Do it.

Action 3: Start a network file. Snippets of information that might be of interest to them can be collected and passed over.

Networks require energizing, give as well as take. What have you done for your network this month?

Examples of information could be:

— *Newspaper articles of interest;*
— *Names in the news;*
— *Books;*
— *Articles;*
— *A helpful contact;*
— *Changes in legislation, such as grants available;*
— *An example of good practice to learn from;*
— *A good idea.*

What can you put in to your networks?

Awareness   There are clearly many ways to grow and develop a business. One way is to take on the market leader or established competitor. If you do it head-on, unless you have competitive advantages recognized by customers, then you will need resources in the ratio of 3 : 1 to have a chance of winning business from the established competitor, i.e. if your competitor has three salesmen then you will need nine or if they spend £10,000 on advertising you will need to spend £30,000. The lesson is not to tackle market leaders head-on (unless you have a strong competitive advantage). Our successful companies have found an alternative: they search for a gap and work through it.

This is how they do it. They spend lots of time with customers (networking). They focus on what they are good at (core skills), and they listen to customers and their problems. A customer problem becomes their opportunity.

Alternatively, they break with convention and do something completely different. They fix the problem quickly, often jointly with the customer. If it is a new customer the process can become problem-seeking/problem-solving, and a friend for life. Let us examine the process a little more closely.

Problems occur when the business is suffering. In the summer of 1991 our customers suffered in the recession. Their main concern was lack of orders. There is no point trying to sell them production training, but they need to know 'How to Create New Business'. Sometimes customers have great difficulty in articulating their problems, and they may not even be aware of the true cause. Here is an opportunity for you. You can help them identify and focus on real problems – these are your opportunities.

One blockage to the process is where you go in selling, i.e. here is the solution: now what is your problem? To make this process work you need to ask questions and listen. Go over the top with the solution: make it memorable.

> **Example:** *One company identified from a customer that they were fed up with suppliers taking forever to get back to them with proposals and quotations. They returned to their office, wrote the proposal, focused the typing resources on it, and returned the proposal personally the same day to the customer. Naturally they won the contract, and the customer still talks about it as an excellent example of customer service.*

In summary the process looks like this:

1. *Network with customers;*
2. *Ask problem-raising questions;*
3. *Identify where the pain exists;*
4. *Fix it quickly;*
5. *Make it memorable;*
6. *Maintain the relationship.*

> **Example:** *Every time a representative visits a customer they have a form to complete which identifies customers' problems. This is circulated to interested parties in our business, so if it's mechanical it goes to the Mechanical Engineers or if electrical then to the Electrical Department. We have a problem-solving meeting weekly where we review our top ten customer problems. It's called the Top Ten Committee. We then prioritize and aim to fix them fast. This has created mega opportunities for us over the past year or so. Bonas Machine Company*

> **Example:** *In 1985 the whole of the retail trade was looking at straight-on display trays. This was an innovation from Marks and Spencer. Sainsbury had a different shelf problem from Tesco. So we went to talk with them and solved a problem for each customer, and ended up with a different configuration of trays. Now that caused us a problem, but it was typical of how we were first in, flexible to their needs. Everybody followed, but Derwent Valley Foods was first. Derwent Valley Foods*

Sometimes customers will not admit to having problems, but most will recognize the need to make improvements. What improvements would you like to see in your business?

The skill is to ask the right questions. These need to be problem-raising questions:

- *If you could improve one thing in your business, what would it be?*
- *What keeps you awake at night?*
- *What is stopping you moving forward?*

I suggest you start with the pain, even if it's not business-related. One consultant gets business by helping senior managers' children with their career choices because this is a concern for them.

Once the problem is identified then the magic is created for customers by responding at record speed. It alleviates the pain, they feel good, and sleep easier in their beds.

Remember:
Problem Seeking → Problem Solving = Friend for Life.

2.3 Problem-seeking/Problem-solving

Assessment

Tick here if this is true for your business

1. *We are good at listening to our customers rather than selling products.* [ ]

2. *We use problem-seeking and problem-solving as major sources of business generation.* [ ]

3. *We help our customers identify real problems.* [ ]

4. *We often surprise our customers with the speed and effectiveness of our problem-solving on their behalf.* [ ]

5. *Our business is flexible enough to respond immediately to major opportunities.* [ ]

6. *We have well proven procedures for problem-seeking.* [ ]

Fewer than four ticks and you need to take *Action.*

2.3 Problem-seeking/Problem-solving

Action   Action 1:   Read Toolkit 3, which is an introduction to the process of problem-seeking/problem-solving. This is the heart of Hallmarks. Circulate it to your customer contact people. Tell them this is how we now do business around here.

Action 2:   Here is how to use the problem-seeking and problem-solving process to create major sales opportunities.

Step 1:   Arrange a meeting with a new or existing customer. Once you have established that you are dealing with a decision-maker say, 'To enable me to really understand your business and how we can best support you, do you mind if I ask you a few questions?' Clearly this process can only be used with the key decision-makers in the buying process. If you find that you are meeting a purchasing clerk (i.e. not the decision-maker) then the way to identify the key people in the buying process without insulting the purchasing clerk is to ask this question: 'If we were to become a supplier to your company what would be the process that we would need to go through to achieve buyer status?' This question will help you identify the right people to meet.

Step 2:   Ask the following questions to seek to identify problems. Use those that suit your style, or invent your own.

       – *What improvements would you like to see in your business?*
       – *What is causing you difficulty right now?*
       – *What one thing would help you sleep easy in your bed?*
       – *What would have the biggest impact on your business?*
       – *Where could you get the best value for money?*
       – *What blockages face you?*
       – *What's stopping you achieving your goals?*

Make up your own problem-seeking questions.

Step 3: Once the customer has flagged up an issue help him or her examine it in detail with the following questions.

       – *What effect is that (problem) having?*
       – *What does your boss think about it?*
       – *What will the long-term effect be?*
       – *What will be the knock-on effect to your customers?*

Again, invent your own problem-probing questions.

Step 4: Say, 'If we could help you resolve that (problem) would you be happy?'

Step 5: Where possible, fix the problem at lightning speed to create customer delight.

Step 6: Develop your relationship and seek more business.

Action 3: Find a theme that is common for customers and go seeking the issue – for example, every organization has problems with training evaluation. So I would ask, 'What problem do you have with evaluation?' (knowing they are bound to have problems).

Problems likely to concern customers are:

1.

2.

3.

4.

5.

Action 4: Develop your own list of problem-seeking questions. Train your people to ask them.

Q1.

Q2.

Q3.

Q4.

Q5.

Action 5: Practise asking questions and listening for clues. Practise staying quiet while customers pour out their concerns. It's hard work, but watch the business flow in!

Action 6: Fix some problems at express speed. Do something in an hour that usually takes you a week. Watch the customer's eyes light up.

List things that would amaze your customers:

1.

2.

3.

4.

5.

Action 7: Share success and ideas with colleagues so they too can delight your customers.

Awareness / **Surprising customers with the level of service you provide**

Customer delight is normally personal; customer service corporate. You know if you are delighting customers by the amount of unsolicited new business they offer you. This is the acid test. Customer service will maintain your customer base and order level, whereas delight, by definition, extends it. If customers are really delighted they normally act on it rather than simply say thank you.

> **Example:** *It's not enough simply to satisfy your customers in today's business world. You have to delight them. You do this by addressing a whole number of areas – personal integrity, quality delivery and that little bit extra. Bonas Machine Company*

It is tough but worth it. It is also different from customer service. Time for some examples.

> **Example:** *A friend ordered some new carpets for a new house. The day they moved in he opened the door to be met by a mountain of off-cuts in the hall. After clearing them away he found all the doors had been taken off so he had to move them into the garage. Eventually, two hours later, he was able to move his furniture.*

Having had that experience, the next time he moved he sought another carpet fitter. This time he opened the door to find not a thread anywhere (Customer Service). The doors had been refitted and opened properly (Customer Service). But the best bit was yet to come. In the kitchen was a small vase with some freesias and a card which read 'Mrs Jones, welcome to your new home – The Carpet Fitter' (Customer Delight). A light-hearted example, yet he could have as much business as he liked, the ladies loved him. They told everybody all the time. He did not need to advertise.

Example: *A customer lived in Scotland but supported Blackpool Football Club. In 1991 Blackpool reached the semi-final of a Cup. He was desperate for a ticket but could not get one. On hearing of this the supplier dispatched a secretary from Sheffield to Blackpool to obtain tickets for the match. They sent them by courier to their customer the same day (perhaps a bit more than customer service at this point). But the best was yet to come. At half-time the customer was welcomed over the Tannoy by name and asked to report to the directors' suite after the match. Awaiting him and his colleague was a bottle of champagne, courtesy of the company, together with a signed photograph of his favourite team as a reminder of the day.*

What are the ingredients in customer delight?

- *Satisfaction beyond the norm;*
- *Spontaneous or unexpected;*
- *Often a personal touch;*
- *Speed;*
- *Attention to detail;*

The results of customer delight are:

- *It surprises people and makes them feel good;*
- *They tell everybody about it;*
- *It leads to more business being offered;*
- *It is offered without the expectation of reciprocation – it is* not *emotional blackmail, it is genuine.*

The challenge is to delight, not embarrass, customers.

Example: *One successful company decided not to attend the industry exhibition at the National Exhibition Centre but to take their customers on the Orient Express. It was a memorable day which everyone enjoyed and the customers spent the next twelve months asking what was happening next? Most important, sales increased from these customers by 16 per cent in the year – well above expectations.*

Customer delight can set new standards and create expectations which are hard to follow. But it's fantastic when it works! It's not enough in today's business to satisfy the customer: what you have to do is delight them.

Example: *Imagine putting your dog into kennels when you go on holiday. They look after your dog excellently. It looks healthy and happy with bright eyes, a wet nose and a shining coat, on your return (customer satisfaction to this point).*

Back at the house there is a postcard from your dog who also claims to have been on holiday! (customer delight). (You see, you are smiling at the prospect.) Also at Christmas you get a card from your dog wishing you a Happy Christmas. Triple A Animal Hotel & Care Centre

---

2.4 Customer Delight

Assessment

1. *We have customer-oriented front-line people.* [ ]

2. *We create a high level of unsolicited repeat business by delighting our customers.* [ ]

3. *Customers often express surprise at the speed of our response.* [ ]

4. *We can provide six good examples of customer delight from our last month's business.* [ ]

5. *Customers' complaints are often turned into delight by the speed and quality of our response.* [ ]

6. *I have experienced customer delight.* [ ]

Fewer than four ticks and you need to take *Action*.

2.4 Customer Delight

Action   You may recall how we defined customer delight.

Customer satisfaction is satisfaction with the performance of a product or service. Customer delight adds personal satisfaction, building the self-esteem of the customer.

Here are some actions to take, but bear in mind that these are examples only. By definition, customer delight is created by personal actions.

Action 1:	Send a personal note thanking someone.
Action 2:	A bottle of champagne when someone is promoted.
Action 3:	The customer's name on a spot in your car park (rather than the director's!).
Action 4:	The customer's name on a tea cup when they visit you.
Action 5:	Your staff send the customer a signed birthday card.
Action 6:	You invite your customer and wife (or husband) out to dinner to celebrate their wedding anniversary.
Action 7:	A card sent from holiday.
Action 8:	Here is a way to link customer delight into your normal customer services activities:
Step 1:	Get a team of four or five of your people together (these do not have to be the top team). Get a flip chart and pen or drawing board.

Step 2:   Draw your normal order/delivery cycle from receiving an enquiry to seeing payment. It might look like this:

Telephone Enquiry	Sales Visit	Quote	Order Placed	Confirmed	Goods Dispatched	After Sales	Payment Received

Step 3:   Brainstorm – where in this cycle can we create customer delight by surprising our customer? Where would we have most impact?

Step 4:   Take action.

2.5 Market development

Awareness Successful companies create a recipe based on their experiences of solving customer problems and use it. They apply this as widely as possible.

'Sticking to the knitting' and focusing on core skills is the way our successful companies developed. Clearly additional skills can be developed over time but our companies do not appear to get involved in developing totally new products or services. They ask the questions: 'Are we making the most of the products and services we already possess? Who else can we sell them to?' The product and service gradually evolves and is slowly shaped by changing customer needs.

Sometimes companies diversify away from their existing products because of boredom. One engineering company in Consett considered (after the MD had a holiday in Florida) opening a hamburger bar in Newcastle. They forgot that McDonalds have a few years' more experience at it. They eventually decided to stick to engineering because the hamburger bar was not part of their core strategy. They had a good product which they sold in the North-East. They now sell it all over the UK and make lots of money.

The way successful companies create more customers is through the establishment of an effective business-generating system (BGS). The purpose of the BGS is to create opportunities to sell and develop new business.

It could be that for one business the BGS is mail-out and telephone follow-up. This might create all the new business. In other businesses it could be attending trade exhibitions. In my business it is presenting papers to conferences. The BGS ensures that we get to sufficient conferences to present enough papers to build our business.

The real issue about BGS is that the channel of communication with your market will be different. The key questions to ask are:

1. *Where do I get my new business from?*
2. *Do I have a system that generates enough new opportunities to meet the business objectives?*

Interestingly, over 90 per cent of our clients consult us for 'Marketing Plans' but really need a system to create new business. The section on *Action* shows you how to set about creating enough opportunities to satisfy your business needs.

Example: *AbleClean of Hartlepool wrote to one of my people thanking him because the business-generating system had increased sales in the first six months by 41 per cent. They originally requested a marketing plan and an idea for diversification.*

DIVERSIFICATION AND TOTALLY NEW PRODUCT IDEAS

Log Sheet

Write all your new ideas here for diversification and new products (where you have little knowledge or expectation).

1.
2.
3.
4.
5.
6.
7.
8.
9.
10.
11.
12.

Now tear it out and burn it!

2.5 Market Development

Assessment

1. *We grow by selling our proven products/services to more customers.*   [   ]

2. *We do not spend major resources on diversification (unless there is no other option).*   [   ]

3. *We plan for and allocate sufficient resources to developing new markets.*   [   ]

4. *We only get involved in bringing new products to market when there is a significant demand.* [   ]

5. *Long-term prospects in our primary markets are excellent.*   [   ]

6. *We have an effective business-generating system to create new business.*   [   ]

Fewer than four ticks and you need to take *Action*.

2.5 Market Development

Action Market development is undertaken not only when existing markets are either saturated or under threat; it should happen constantly.

> **Action 1:** Assess the opportunities for greater market share. How big are they? What is your share? What does the future look like? What threats (if any) exist?
>
> **Action 2:** Identify the next natural step for your business. Successful companies often develop their markets geographically.

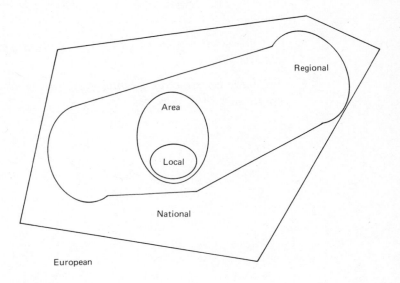

What is your next natural market extension?

Action 3:	Create a resource (person) to develop a network for your next step. Find out who supplies? What is the potential? Who are the key contacts?
	Remember the skills required to build a new network are different from those of maintaining an existing network.
Action 4:	Develop an effective business-generating system using the process that follows:

Buying Customers: Sales target × Production lead time.

Working Prospects: Monthly sales target × Conversion rate of enquiries.

Market Potential: Working platform × Conversion Rate × 'Thinking leadtime' in months.

Step 1:	Calculate target annual sales.
Step 2:	Calculate average order size from historical records.
Step 3:	Calculate number of orders required for year.

$$\text{Calculation:} \quad \frac{\text{Step 1}}{\text{Step 2}} = \text{No. of orders}$$

Step 4:	Decide how many orders will come from existing customers (Buying customers).
Step 5:	Determine how many new orders are required.

Calculation: Step 3 – Step 4 = New orders required

Step 6:	Calculate conversion rate
	Quotes to orders (e.g. three quotes to one order)
Step 7:	Calculate the number of new orders required.

Calculation: multiply Step 5 by Step 6

	At this point divide the answer by 12. This gives new orders per month. Build in any seasonality (e.g. no orders at Christmas).
Step 8:	Determine the conversion rate of new prospects to quotes (e.g. four new prospects to one quotation).
Step 9:	Calculate number of prospects required.
	Calculations: multiply Step 7 by Step 8. Divide by 12 to obtain monthly figure.

This is the arithmetic of the BGS. Now you need to work out how to create the business on a regular basis. This time work from Step 9.

Step 10:	Determine how new prospects are best created in your business (i.e. mailshots, telephone calls, advertisements, exhibitions, etc.).
	Plan to undertake this activity monthly to create the level of prospects required at Step 9. (You can use the worksheet provided overleaf on p. 98.)

Business Generating System Worksheet

A.   Determine last year's turnover   --------

B.   Determine total number of orders last year   --------

C.   Determine how many orders came from repeat business (existing customers)   --------

D.   Calculate percentage of repeat business $(C \div B) \times 100$ --------

E.   Calculate average order size $(A \div B)$ --------

F.   Establish next year's target turnover   --------

G.   Calculate total number of orders required next year $(F \div E)$ --------

H.   Determine number of repeat business expected $(G \times D)$ --------

I.   Calculate number of extra orders needed from new customers $(G - H)$ --------

J.   Determine how many quotations sent out last year and how many won.   ---in---

K.   Determine how many potential customers visited and how many asked you to quote   ---in---

L.   Calculate how many extra quotations needed to be sent out to new customers $(I \times$ Ratio J$)$ --------

M.   Calculate how many potential new customers need to be identified $(L \times$ Ratio K$)$ --------

3.1
Structure/
roles

3.5
Support
network
partnerships

3.2
Customer
partnerships

**HALLMARK 3:
Partnering**

3.4
Supplier
partnerships

3.3
Staff
partnerships

Creating and maintaining partnerships with everyone who affects your business is a Hallmark of succesful companies. This chapter shows you how to develop profitable partnerships.

This process is defined as working in partnership with people who affect your business.

Working in partnership involves the creative talents and energies of everyone who can affect your business. The effect is that everyone, from staff through to supplier and customers, works together for mutual gain. This process adds real value by avoiding adverse relationships and recognizing that success comes from long-term commitments and not short-term 'deals'. This section shows you how to partner successfully.

Awareness / Adding value to the organization it serves

Your organization structure should be designed to support your business plan. This is of crucial importance. If you are extending your markets does your organization structure support this aim? Have staff enough time to focus on the opportunities? One company planned to go into Europe. The owner told me he would get to it when he had time among his other priorities. (Rate their chances of making it happen quickly and effectively on a scale of 1–10.)

You obviously have choices about how you organize. Without exception, our successful companies structure their business to support their business plan and, most importantly, to keep their people close to customers.

One problem that growth and success can bring is how you structure your business. The temptation is to add more levels as you employ more people. Therefore as you grow you can move away from the customers. The entrepreneur becomes an administrator. This is so important it is worthy of elaboration.

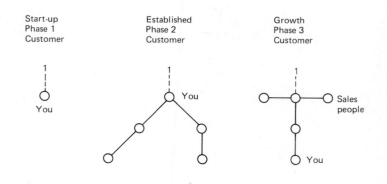

A Phase 1 business stays close to the customer because there are few choices! You know the customers personally because *you* are dealing with them all the time. At Phase 2 you grow in size and take on more people. You have choices. You can maintain your customer contacts or delegate them.

If customers have a relationship with you which is the primary reason they buy, then stick with it. If they don't, then you can delegate.

At Phase 3 the choices are more difficult. As you grow, inevitably more people are contacting customers. The crucial choice is where you fit in.

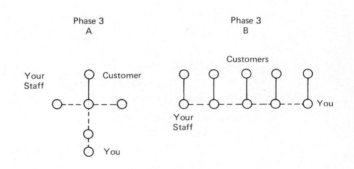

Phase 3A is the classic growth structure. The entrepreneur becomes the manager and stops seeing customers. Phase 3B is an alternative. The entrepreneur continues his customer contacts while other people develop their own customers.

Many companies who are successful operate a phase 3B structure. How are you structured, Phase 3A or 3B?

Phase 3B allows the key players to travel and maintain customer contact. They are not desk-bound running meetings and sending memos. But it is necessary to work harder at lateral information flow, to prevent overlap. Our experience shows the benefits are worth the effort.

Having thought about your structure and ensured that it supports the business plan the next step is to consider what people in the structure do to build partnerships. The concept of partnering extends beyond customers to every key contact that affects your business, both internal and external.

How do partnerships work? Here are some guidelines:

Commitment:	*The reason the partners are working together must be important enough to get people involved. It cannot be half-hearted.*
Win-win:	*The aim must be mutual benefit for both sides in the partnership. One must not be seen to be constantly gaining at the expense of the other.*
Long-term view:	*Partnerships are long-term, between stable organizations; short-term relationships are not partnerships.*
Openness:	*Both partners should keep each other informed. Surprises can be deadly.*
Development of trust:	*Trust does not happen quickly. It takes time to develop.*
Effective representation:	*Both sides need a champion to marshal resources and make things happen.*
Integration:	*Both sides need to be integrated and supplied with information and systems.*

The key is, then, to make these principles work in practice. How can you support this process? Do you build effective partnerships?

3.1 Structure/Roles

Assessment

Tick here if this is true for your business

1. *Our organization structure supports our business plan.* [ ]

2. *Our organization structure ensures the right people stay as close as possible to our customers.* [ ]

3. *Starting from scratch and given a clean sheet of paper, we would create exactly the same structure as we have right now.* [ ]

4. *We aim to build partnerships with all our key people.* [ ]

5. *Our business is built on partnership principles.* [ ]

6. *Partnerships are intrinsic to our business success.* [ ]

Fewer than four ticks and you need to take *Action*.

3.1 Structure/Roles

Action Action 1: Start with a clean sheet of paper and consider your future plans. Forget your existing business. What structure would ideally serve your future plans? Draw this on a sheet of paper. Compare this to your existing situation. What does this tell you? Take action to prepare for the future. Redraw the chart. Take out levels. Get key people closer to your customers.

Action 2: Redraw your structure to enable you to spend at least 30% of your time with customers.

Action 3: Publish your structure so that people know where they fit.

Action 4: Get your top people together. Discuss the idea of partnering. What kinds of partnerships would make sense for us? How well do we manage our partnerships?

List your partnerships.	Tick which are effective/ not effective	
	+	−
1.	[ ]	[ ]
2.	[ ]	[ ]
3.	[ ]	[ ]
4.	[ ]	[ ]
5.	[ ]	[ ]
6.	[ ]	[ ]

Strengthen pluses and turn minuses into pluses.

Action 5:   Keep a time log for a week. See how much time is *actually* spent in partnerships.

Assessment / Adding value to your customer's business

'People buy people first' *Metro FM*

A test of the quality of your customer partnerships is the level of repeat business you get. The acid test is when you mess up and let your customer down and still keep the business. It is as simple as this: the better the quality of your partnership with your customer the more business you will get from them. The only exception to this rule is where you have a really unique product that is unavailable elsewhere.

How do you develop customer partnerships? Here is the best method I know.

1. *Decide how you like to be treated as a customer.*
2. *Compare this with how you treat your best customer.*
3. *Repeat Steps 1 and 2 with customers covering 80 per cent of your business.*

> **Example:** *Yes, we know them (customers) very well. We build relationships; if we can't build a relationship with a customer we think hard about whether we want the business. We have very good customer relationships. Cresstale*

Very often when we have conducted customer perception surveys for our clients the concerns expressed by customers are about the lack of partnership. Typical comments would be:

- *'We only hear from you when you are chasing orders – you never contact us at other times.'*
- *'It is not that you delivered late, it is the fact you did not let us know.'*
- *'We do not have a name to contact when we have queries.'*
- *'You never return our calls promptly.'*
- *'You seem to operate in the belief that, "It would be a good business if it was not for our customers."'*
- *'We never feel confident that we can trust you.'*

If we treated our best friends in similar ways, would they stay around for long?

It seems to me that the real meanings behind these very common complaints are:

- *You don't communicate with us.*
- *You do not treat us with any respect.*
- *There is no relationship, we are just a sale to you.*
- *You do nothing to build our self-esteem – in fact, quite the opposite.*

Example: *One company was surprised that a competitor came along and offered their customer of five years' standing the same product at a few pounds less and took away their business. The chairman told me he was shocked and felt let down. I asked about the quality of the partnership with the customer. He told me he thought it was OK because they had had few written complaints over the years.*

There is a difference between relationships and partnerships, which is illustrated by Level 1 and Level 2 below.

Level 1: Customer Relationships
The starting-point is to treat customers like friends. One salesman in our research suggested, 'My objective on any

first call is to get an invite back.' This seems a good starting-point. His second objective was, 'To understand my customers' business as well as they do.' Again a superb objective. One starts a relationship, the other consolidates it. Beyond that, follow the maxim, treat my customers like my best friends. The benefit will be long-term business relationships.

Level 2: Partnerships
Building partnerships with customers goes beyond simple courtesies of communication and treating them with respect. It requires you to find ways of adding value to your customers' business for them. My salesman friend again had a view of this: 'I build real partnerships by helping my customers add value to their business. I need to understand the needs of my customer's customer.'

One small independent brewery gets its sales team to help publicans with their merchandising. This helps the publican to sell more products and make more money. Most of their competitors simply take orders. Guess who gets the business?

How can you add value to your customers' business?

The ideal partnership is synergistic. You are able to contribute to a degree that helps them improve their business and hence they buy even more from you. This result is long-term commitment.

Research by a UK business has established that it costs as much as three times the amount to create a new customer as to keep an existing one. Creating partnerships is not simply altruistic, it is sound commercial sense.

Start a relationship	–	*Aim to be invited back.*
Maintain a relation-ship	–	*Understand your customers' business better than they do.*
Create a partnership	–	*Understand your customers' customer in order to help them add real value to their business.*

WHY CUSTOMERS QUIT!

1% die

3% move away

5% develop other friendships

9% for competitive reasons

14% because of product dissatisfaction

68% quit because of . . .

ATTITUDE OF INDIFFERENCE
TOWARDS CUSTOMER BY SUPPLIER

Assessment

1. *The quality of our customer partnerships is our major business strength.*   [ ]

2. *We enjoy a high level of repeat business and referrals.*   [ ]

3. *Some of our key customers are our best friends.*   [ ]

4. *We aim to understand our customers' business better than they do.*   [ ]

5. *We add real value to our customers' business by working in partnership.*   [ ]

6. *We build partnerships by trying to understand our customers' customers.*   [ ]

Fewer than four ticks and you need to take *Action*.

3.2 Customer Partnerships

Action Action 1: Give your home telephone number to your key customers.

Action 2: Find out your key customers' main interests. Take them to an event, give them tickets, do something exciting for them.

Action 3: Ring your key customers daily/weekly/ monthly (whichever is appropriate), regardless of the level of business.

Action 4: Take your key customers out for a drink – find out about them, their interests, hobbies, ambitions, hopes, fears. Build a friendship. Your aim is *not* to talk shop.

Action 5: Give out some free samples. You may take your product for granted, your customer won't.

Action 6: Think further about building partnerships with your customers. Are they hurting? What can you do to help? How can you help them add value to their business?

Key customers	Current problems	Where we can help
1.		
2.		
3.		
4.		
5.		

6.

7.

8.

9.

10.

Action 7: Agree to talk to some of your customers'
customers. Make a list of their needs. Talk to
your customers about how you can help them.
Action 8: Photocopy WHY CUSTOMERS QUIT (p.111) and
put it on your notice boards.

Awareness / Creating mutually beneficial contracts

> **Example:** *I once had a boss who could get me to walk through brick walls for him. I had another who could not motivate me to get out of bed in the morning.*
>
> *A simple illustration – the annual appraisal. Picture the situation. I was invited into the boss's office. He instructed his secretary to hold all calls and make us coffee. We sat around a low coffee-table, jackets off, ties loosened. He informed me that he had been giving considerable thought to me and my job. He appeared to have made copious notes. He told me how he appreciated my work. I noticed he had put one of my reports up to the chairman with my name still on it and an attached note, 'David has done a superb job on this project.' He told me he had investigated some development opportunities and had talked to a business school, and gave me a prospectus for an MBA. He had cleared it with the chairman, got the funds and paved the way. He finished the appraisal like this: 'David, it's Ellen's (my partner) birthday on Saturday. Take her out to dinner on us.' He was like this all the time. . . . If he rang me tomorrow (and I haven't seen him in twenty years) and asked me to go to London at 6 a.m. the following day, my answer would be, 'Tony, do you want me to run with a sack of coal on my back via Glasgow?'*
>
> *I also learnt a few lessons from my next boss. He used to call me Richard. . . . All my reports to the chairman had my name whited out and replaced by*

Most managers are familiar with the theory of getting the best from people and building staff relationships. Like many aspects of management, putting the theory into practice is the key problem. It is a particular challenge for fast growth businesses, however, because external customer delight is provided by effective employees, the internal customers. How you treat your people will directly impact on your customers. How effective are your human assets?

There are many books on motivation. I personally have a problem with the concept. Fifty years of research into motivation has failed to produce motivated people. Perhaps we cannot motivate others. Maybe we can only provide incentives. My incentive from Tony was the promise of the MBA. If I performed well I also got to take my partner out to dinner at the company's expense. What incentives do you offer your people?

Example: *One of the companies in our survey rewarded a junior clerk for exceptional performance by buying her and her friend two tickets to see 'New Kids on the Block'. They arranged transport to and from the concert and even checked with her mother that she did not mind her daughter being kept out late. A memorable night for the young lady.*

Would your people run to London via Glasgow with a sack of coal on their back for you or do they disappear like lightning at 5 o'clock?

Building staff relationships requires attention to a simple model.

1. *Recruit the right people.*
2. *Give them clear objectives.*
3. *Train them where necessary.*
4. *Review their performance. Communicate continually, providing feedback.*
5. *Reward good and punish poor performance.*

These five steps will enable you to build a relationship with your people and provide good performance for your business.

There are many ways of enhancing employee relationships. Here are some examples.

- *Providing business cards for everyone, including juniors.*
- *Pictures of staff in reception.*
- *A Christmas bonus in which the highest paid receive the same as the lowest.*
- *Same job titles for everyone – e.g. partner.*

Example: *Keepmoat set out to raise £50,000 during 1991 for an appeal for the blind. They asked the staff to organize 'It's a knockout' over a weekend. People worked 24 hours a day. The appeal raised over £70,000, involved everybody in the business and was a tremendous team-building success. Incidentally, the MD put himself in the stocks to have wet sponges thrown at him by employees. Now that is the meaning of building relationships.*

If you want to create partnerships with your people you need to add a few more steps to the 1–5 basic model outlined above. The benefits will be extra performance, with people taking personal responsibility for getting the job done. This requires leadership. A friend of mine, Gerry Egan, defines leadership *as the ability to produce results beyond expectations.*

Example: *A salesman responded quickly by getting a quote back to the customer the same day. He wins the order and high praise from the boss. But who typed the quote in their lunch-break? Were they recognized and rewarded? Would they do it again next time?*

Leadership requires the building of partnerships with your people in order to produce results beyond expectations. Management is the norm, leadership is exceptional. How do you create partnerships?

Steps 1–5 in our simple model is one-way, i.e., boss → employee.

Step 6 takes the first five steps and makes them two-way. So partnerships are created by managers taking steps 1–5 seriously but being prepared to have them applied to themselves! In other words, the employee sets the boss objectives, suggests timings, provides feedback and takes them out to dinner! The process is two-way, a true partnership. Radical, yes. But the old ways have failed and it is time to try some new ideas.

Example: *Yes, we are very people-orientated here. Our accounts go out the front door if we aren't. There are no accounts on the balance sheet. They are all people. We are a people business and the success of this management team is its ability to deal with people, Metro FM*

3.3 Staff Partnerships

Assessment

1. *Our people give 110 per cent.*   [ ]

2. *Our people provide us with a competitive advantage.*   [ ]

3. *We operate on a true partnership business with our people.*   [ ]

4. *We have the right people to take our business forward.*   [ ]

5. *We have a clear set of incentives for our staff that encourages that bit of extra commitment.* [ ]

6. *Our people take responsibility and produce results beyond our expectations.* [ ]

Fewer than four ticks and you need to take *Action*.

3.3 Staff Partnerships

Action Action 1:   Analyse your human assets as a preliminary to developing partnerships.

Step 1:   Plot each of your key people in the framework below.
Note: This framework considers only value to the business and should not demean people.

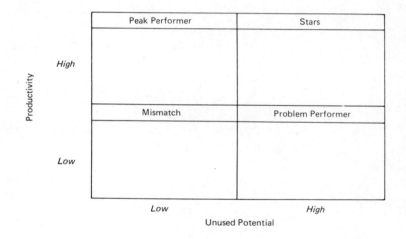

Step 2:   Key Questions:

- *If you found this difficult to do, how well do you know your people?*
- *Who are you going to build partnerships with? Hopefully your stars and your peak performers. You need to sort out your problem performers and deal with any mismatches.*

Action 2: Test your people management system against our five-step model. How effective is your system of staff management?

Action 3: Introduce some new incentives for your people, find out what turns them on and then provide it.

Action 4: Ask your people to review your performance. Start the process of leadership today!

What do I do well?	*What do I do badly?*
1.	1.
2.	2.
3.	3.
4.	4.
5.	5.
6.	6.

What should I improve?	*What training should I undertake?*
1.	1.
2.	2.
3.	3.
4.	4.
5.	5.
6.	6.

Action 5: Set your staff objectives and review these every quarter using the format outlined above.

Action 6: Do something memorable for your people, such as:

- *give them all business cards;*
- *take them out to dinner;*
- *listen to them;*
- *take them with you on joint visits;*
- *tell them about your high-level meetings and dealings.*

Awareness / Ensuring supplies

> **Example:** *We also visited and made presentations to our key suppliers because suppliers are a major element of our financial resources. We tell them about our plans, how our sales are going, keep them informed about what we are trying to do. We made commitments to them about payment, so when we said we wanted a delivery, there was one. They were more willing to help us develop our business and getting credit was no problem. They helped us over the humps and bumps. Derwent Valley Foods*

> *We have a lot of specialist arrangements with suppliers. We go for single sourcing whenever we can. We enter three-year agreements with them. This enables us to control cost and quality and operate tight delivery schedules. We work in partnership to the benefit of both parties. Bonas Machine Company*

Successful companies treat their suppliers as an integral part of their business. It is difficult to see any difference between the way they treat customers, staff or suppliers. They all have similar characteristics:

- *Long-term view;*
- *Two-way benefits;*

- *Win-win relationships;*
- *Mutual respect and trust;*
- *High performance standard;*
- *On-going communications;*
- *Reduction of 'surprises' on both sides.*

Clearly, just as these companies problem-solve for their customers, suppliers are encouraged to do the same for them.

Neat Ideas management undertook a strategic training programme. They encouraged a major supplier to undertake the same training to ensure he supplied them adequately.

Successful companies build 'teams' of staff, customers and suppliers working together. They do not operate in isolation, letting customers down and kicking suppliers.

How do you build partnerships with your supplier? Clearly supplier partnerships ensure continuous supplies.

Example: *One company sends their cheques with orders. Crazy? Until you realize that the supplier stockholds and the company gets a three-hour delivery service guaranteed. Guess who gets the best service if the supplier is really pushed? In addition, the supplier provides many new product opportunities and ideas. 'They are almost part of our own business.'*

3.4 Supplier Partnerships

Assessment

1. *We have long-term contracts with our suppliers.* [ ]

2. *We continuously communicate our plans and requirements to our suppliers.* [ ]

3. *We treat our suppliers as we treat our customers.* [ ]

4. *Our suppliers are an integral part of our business to the extent that they support our competitive thrust.* [ ]

5. *We encourage our suppliers to develop in line with our plans.* [ ]

6. *Our suppliers suggest ideas and innovations that help us develop our business.* [ ]

Fewer than four ticks and you need to take *Action*.

3.4 Supplier Partnerships

Action **Action 1:**   Carry out a supplier attitude survey. What do they think of us as customers?

    Step 1:   Ask them:

- *What do you look for in customers?*
- *Do we match up?*
- *How do we treat you as a supplier?*
- *How could we work in partnership?*
- *What could you contribute to our business?*

    Step 2:   Analyse the results.

- *How can we create partnerships?*
- *How can we derive greater mutual benefit?*
- *What value can your suppliers add to your business in terms of:*
  - *ideas*
  - *products*
  - *solutions to problems*
  - *information*
  - *money*

Action 2:   Consider introducing a supplier of the year award. Announce the winner publicly.

Action 3:   Invite your suppliers into your business, show them how their products work in your process. Ask how they could help improve your business.

Action 4:   Communicate your plans to your key suppliers. Ask for their help in developing your business.

Action 5: Consider entering long-term deals with key suppliers in order to guarantee a supply of key resources.

Awareness / Ensuring your support network adds value

Support networks are those individuals and organizations that are available to develop and assist your business, outside the direct relationships we have already discussed. The most obvious ones are:

- *Accountants;*
- *Bank managers;*
- *Solicitors;*
- *Shareholders;*
- *Family.*

As a general rule you will be contacting these key people (including, I hope, your family) regularly. For example, most bank managers assume no news is bad news. Therefore you do need to be active in contacting them. Bank managers are people too. They are often happy to be given a tour of your business, to be introduced to your team, and to be treated as an important stakeholder rather than as a necessary evil.

You should negotiate regularly with your bank about overdraft rates, bank charges and the level of collateral required. A friend told me he was paying 1.5 per cent over base rate for his overdraft and we were paying 3 per cent. I went back to the bank and in two seconds they reduced our rate to 2 per cent. I asked why they hadn't reduced the rate previously and their reply was that I had not asked! From that day I learnt about negotiating with my bank. Take the initiative and do the same.

Clearly, your family is crucial to supporting your business. Sir John Harvey Jones always made sure he attended his

127

wife's and children's birthday parties. Now if the Chairman of one of the largest UK companies can make time, so can I, and so can you!

> **Example:** *I think one of the most important aspects of our business is the support we have had from our wives and children. Otherwise we couldn't do it. We get absolutely no negative vibrations at all; in fact the opposite, nothing but encouragement. Bonas Machine Company*

There is a conundrum in running a business. If you are successful the business will become all-consuming. If you meet problems you need to work night and day to overcome them. Either way the potential losers can be your family and friends. You need to plan a balance between work and home. Easy in theory – hard in practice.

Other support networks can sometimes get overlooked.

Training and Enterprise Councils (TECs) have funds available for training and expertise. Talk to them (LECs in Scotland).

The Department of Trade and Industry (DTI) has an Enterprise Initiative for independent companies. This includes many grants, especially if you are considering entering into Europe.

Chambers of Commerce have expertise available as well as access to many networks. Call them.

One of the problems about running an independent business is that it can get lonely. However, there is no need to do it all yourself. There are people with funds, expertise and networks available: make them work for you.

3.5 Support Network Partnerships

Assessment

*Tick here if this
is true for your
business*

1. *Our support network is clearly defined and well managed.* [ ]

2. *Our support network adds value to our business.* [ ]

3. *We make space to spend time with our families and friends.* [ ]

4. *We are aware of, and have accessed, grants and expertise available to our business.* [ ]

5. *Our bank manager gets regular information and contact from us.* [ ]

6. *We take advantage of our support network.* [ ]

Fewer than four ticks and you need to take *Action.*

3.5 Support Network Partnerships

Action

Action 1: Draw a diagram of your support network relationships. Example:

Consider your relationship with each member of your network. Do they add value to your business or do they have a negative impact? Mark each with + or −, or if they don't know, =.

Visit each person in your network. Talk to them about your vision for the business. What help can they provide? Find out who are on your side (+) or who are fence sitters (=).

Action 2: Put your partner's and children's birthdays and anniversaries in your diary. Underline in red and plan for them.

Action 3: Invite your bank manager to visit your operation. Treat him like a customer. Introduce him to people. Agree what information you will provide monthly. Negotiate about your overdraft, bank charges and guarantees.

Action 4: Contact your local TEC and DTI office. Find out what training, support, advice or grants may be available.

Action 5: Get your accountants involved. Tell them you are tired of simply paying for audits; you want ten good ideas. Tell them you are considering changing your accountant!

Accountants' good ideas. (Ask them to fill this in!)

1.

2.

3.

4.

5.

6.

7.

8.

9.

10.

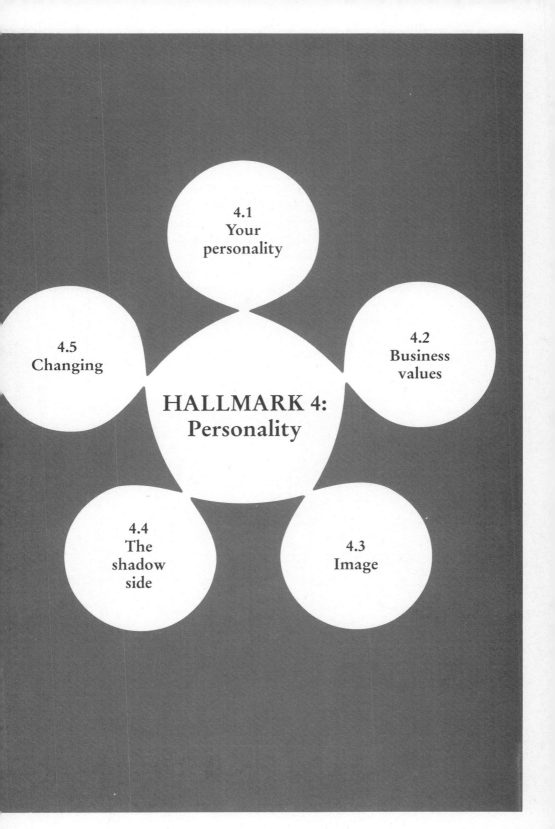

4.1
Your
personality

4.5
Changing

4.2
Business
values

HALLMARK 4:
Personality

4.4
The
shadow
side

4.3
Image

Personality is the perceived character of the business, both internally and externally. Internally, personality creates common commitment to the vision. Externally, it provides an image to your customers. Either way, it is too important to be left to chance. Success companies *manage* their personality.

Personality is the 'soft side' of the business which is not often discussed, particularly by hard-nosed and practical business people, but which has such an impact on the effectiveness of your business that it cannot be ignored.

Managed personality means taking actions internally so that the external face is positive. The challenge as businesses grow and develop is to ensure that the quality of image and personality is not diluted and tarnished. Successful companies appear to be able to drive the business values into the heart of the organization, thus ensuring that a positive external image is maintained. This section explains how to manage personality effectively.

Awareness / Knowing yourself in order to understand your business

It has been said that the personality of the business owner and the business itself are the same. In other words, your strengths and weaknesses are mirrored in the strengths and weaknesses of your business. I have come to the conclusion that this is true of both large and small businesses. Can you really separate the personality of Richard Branson from Virgin or Anita Roddick from Bodyshop?

Understanding your own strengths and weaknesses can be the first step in becoming more aware of the strengths and weaknesses of your business. There are many ways of achieving this aim. You could ask your people what you are really like, or you could try psychometric tests like:

- *OPQ5* (Saville Holdsworth), which will tell you about your personality.*
- *Belbin†, which will tell you about your team style.*
- *Myers Briggs‡, which will tell you how you relate to others, and your decision-making style.*

This information can help you define your strengths and minimise your weaknesses and, as a result, those of your business. Personality tests are very user-friendly these days and can be administered by consultants to provide very helpful insights.

---

* Saville and Holdsworth Ltd, The Old Post House, 81 High Street, Esher, Surrey KT10 9QA.
† Belbin Associates Ltd, The Burleigh Business Centre, 52 Burleigh Street, Cambridge CB1 1DJ.
‡ Katherine C Briggs and Isabel Myers Briggs, Consultancy Psychology Press Inc, 577 College Avenue, Palo Alto, California 94306.

> **Example:** *A managing director was identified as a 'plant' (ideas person) on the Belbin questionnaire. Her personal organization skills were awful and the business going nowhere slowly.*
>
> *She appointed a managing director from within who was a 'co-ordinator/shaper' and she became chairman responsible for new products (ideas). Turnover tripled in two years as the business became co-ordinated and controlled. She was happy because she was making the best use of her strengths. She was also pleased with the business results and was seeing the business flourish.*

The personality of the key players is influential to business success in other ways. People take their lead from you. A most important role for top management is to help the organization develop by setting examples through their own behaviour as 'role models'.

Not all staff are familiar with the business plan in black and white, but by observing the actions of top management people learn what is valued and expected and adjust their behaviour and priorities accordingly. This is particularly true where customer service is important: it is difficult to describe but easy to observe, experience and copy.

Symbolic actions are very important for role models to consider. If top management are committed to increasing the quality of customer service at the 'sharp end' they might spend some time themselves actually undertaking customer service activities rather than issuing edicts and memos.

> **Example:** *A managing director in one company ordered a batch of products to be publicly burnt because he found a defective item. After that everyone understood that quality mattered.*

Clearly these actions reinforce the mission and vision. In this case the mission was to produce high-quality components. The symbolic action of publicly burning the products reinforced the mission in a very powerful manner. It is these actions and anecdotes which have a more powerful influence on people's behaviour than any business plan. The inference is clear. The key role of top management is about *doing* things and not just saying that things will be done.

How you spend your time is a clear signal to your business about the real business priorities. Someone said it is not that they (the staff) don't notice what we do, it is the fact that they do!

4.1 Your Personality

Assessment

Tick here if this is true for your business

1. *I manage my time very effectively and act as a role model for our staff.* [ ]

2. *I understand my own strengths and weaknesses and use this information to advantage in our business.* [ ]

3. *I behave in line with the business priorities, sending the right signals to my people.* [ ]

4. *We have many symbols that reinforce our key business objectives.* [ ]

5. *I have a clear set of personal values that guide our decision-making.* [ ]

6. *We have undertaken psychometric tests in our business and use this information to build on strengths and minimize weaknesses.* [ ]

Fewer than four ticks means you need to take *Action*.

4.1 Your Personality

Action

Action 1: Undertake some psychometric tests to find out more about your personal strengths and weaknesses. There is a contact where you can obtain information on qualified test providers:

The British Psychological Society
St Andrews House
48 Princess Road East
Leicester LE1 7DR

Adjust your role in your business to accommodate your strengths.

Action 2: Ask your key internal people to appraise your job performance. What do they perceive to be your strengths and weaknesses? This is much better done 'on the run' than by the bureaucratic annual appraisal system.

Action 3: Keep a time log in your diary to discover what messages you are giving your business. Does your use of time match your business priorities?

Action 4: Try some symbolic actions to reinforce the priorities of your business: if customer care is a key issue, for example, go and contribute at the front line for a day. If a letter of thanks is received for the work of an employee, celebrate it publicly.

Action 5: How do you spend your time? To determine the message you are giving to your people about how you value customers, estimate on average how many hours a week you spend on the following:

1. *Personally with customers*   ------
2. *Cutting costs*   ------
3. *Visiting your own people in the field*   ------
4. *Talking to other managers*   ------
5. *Learning what customers think of your service*   ------
6. *In meetings*   ------
7. *Finding out what your customers want*   ------
8. *Making technical improvements*   ------
9. *Joint visits to customers*   ------
10. *Recognizing employees who perform well*   ------

Scoring
A   Total for odd-numbered
    items (1,3,5,7,9)   ------
B   Total for even-numbered
    items (2,4,6,8,10)   ------

Interpretation
Your total A time is that which you spend on customer care.
B time is not directly related to customers. If your A time is
higher the message to your people is that customers count.
What kind of role model do you provide for your business?

Awareness / The set of criteria used for making decisions

Business values are the inner aspects, the fundamental character of the business – in other words, the core values and
the mission. Image is the external face which the business
presents to the world.

Successful businesses have a clear set of business values
that permeates everything they do. Many of the values have
been covered in other chapters, but examples are:

- *Customers come first in all our dealings.*
- *We are committed to spending the maximum amount of
  time with our customers.*
- *We value quality of product and customer service.*
- *We provide good products/services and can charge pre-
  mium prices.*
- *We personally get involved in the action, we are not
  desk-bound.*
- *We treat all our key influences – staff, customers,
  suppliers – with the utmost integrity.*
- *Our people are our greatest asset.*

The difference between the successful companies and the rest
is simply this: the successful companies say the right words
and translate them into action continuously; the less successful ones may say the right words, but that is all.

Chairman's statement:	Training is important to our business.
Employee:	*Can I do a training course?*
Boss:	No.
Employee:	*Can I fund it myself and have time off?*
Boss:	No.
Employee:	*Why?*
Boss:	You might leave if we train you.
Employee:	*But what about the chairman's statement: 'Training is important to our business'?*
Boss:	That's the kind of stupid thing chairmen say.

Values are much more than lip service. They are the core philosophy of the business. They can:

- *Define the fundamental character of the business;*
- *Create a sense of identity;*
- *Determine how resources will be allocated;*
- *Reduce confusion and game-playing;*
- *Provide guidelines for implementing company plans.*

The promise on the cover of this book is 'Successful Business.' What is a good business? One definition is that it:

- *provides good financial returns to shareholders;*
- *delights customers;*
- *creates committed employees.*

It may also be one which has integrity in all its dealings. It has a personality that it can live with. A character it is proud of. It behaves in an ethical and moral way as well as being successful.

Somehow you know when you or your business is not behaving in line with your business values. It does not feel quite right. It causes you to think and you sense it is out of order.

Example: *One company states in all its literature that it is non-sexist. Why does it not have women in management positions?*

Example: *The MD of one small business cannot remember the name of the receptionist but continually talks about how important everyone is in his business.*

4.2 Business Values

Assessment

*Tick here if this
is true for your
business*

1. *We have a clear set of business values that guide our decision-making.*   [ ]

2. *Our actions are consistent with our business values.*   [ ]

3. *Our values are consistently reflected by top management.*   [ ]

4. *Everybody in our business understands our values.*   [ ]

5. *We take account of our values when we develop our plans.*   [ ]

6. *We have a 'good' business that behaves with integrity.*   [ ]

Fewer than four ticks and you need to take *Action*.

4.2 Business Personality

Action   Action 1:   Write down your core business values. Discuss them with your key people. Are your business decisions in line with these values? What do you need to do to move your business back into line with your values?

Step 1:   List your core values.

1.

2.

3.

4.

5.

Step 2:   Discuss these with your people.

Step 3:   List decisions in line with these values.

1.

2.

3.

4.

5.

Step 4: Consider if you need to take corrective action – for example, Steps 1 and 3 do not line up. Actions to be taken.

1.

2.

3.

4.

5.

Action 2: Check out the business values of your people, your suppliers and your customers. Are these the people you really want to build partnerships with?

4.3
Image

Awareness / The management of the external identity of your business

Image is the clothes you wear – what the world sees. It's what people say about you when you are not there! People make judgements about us all the time whether we like it or not. Our image can either be managed or left to chance. Successful companies are careful about maintaining a certain image with their customers. They leave nothing to chance.

One of the difficulties with image is that it is how we are perceived by others, *not* as we see ourselves. So how do we know? Well, you can ask people either informally or through your customer attitude survey. Hopefully, your external image will match with how you want to be seen – not like the following example:

Self-image	*Customer Perception*
Innovative	Stable
Progressive	Modern
Professional	Professional
Customer-focused	Product-focused
Top end of the market	Mid-market
Well priced	Expensive
Confident	Confident
Future-oriented	Stuck in the present

Clearly our friend has some image problems here!

> **Example:** *In 1984 we developed a logo and a letter-head. We reviewed this in 1990 after our design consultant produced some research which showed that our image was that of an early 80s computer software business. At the time the logos were 'in' and the typeface modern. However, in six years we had grown and changed rapidly and our image did not match the current business personality.*

> **Example:** *Company image had been a core feature with Ace from the beginning. Ace was chosen as a name because of its alphabetical listing benefit and to represent being No. 1 with the association of having a quality aim.*
>
> *A red diamond in the logo denotes quality and money — key elements of business success. The other card suits were not suitable as they are identified with death, risk and romance. Ace Conveyors*

Image is not all about advertisements. It is created by every message you send to the world. One delivery business gets its staff to answer the telephone on the first ring. Customers' impressions: this is a well organized outfit – I would trust them to perform.

When I first started in business I called my house 'Melrose House'; I thought this sounded better to clients than 13 Arcadia Avenue!

> **Example:** *Superior Cleaning Specialists dressed all its staff in blue overalls because its major customer, British Telecom, at the time was trying to convince the world that the image of dog mess and graffiti in its public phone boxes was simply not true. They wanted their cleaners to be visible and present the right image.*

Image management is not about conning people into believing you are what you aren't, but simply that you are seen as you want to be. One company told me that they thought it unethical to manage their image; people had to take them as they found them. Frankly, as a customer I found them rude, arrogant and disorganized. I wonder what their other customers thought? How do your customers find you? What image do you portray to your world?

> **Example:** *Some months ago my partner required some electrical work undertaking at home. She called an electrician from Yellow Pages. 'I'll be there at 6 o'clock.' What time did he arrive? 9 o'clock. He walked straight over the carpet in the hall with mud spilling from his boots. 'Can I borrow a ruler and a pencil?', he enquired, as he extinguished his cigarette in the sink.*
>
> *She tried another company. 'I'll be there at 5 pm.' At 5 pm precisely the doorbell rang. My God, she thought, somebody turning up on time, this is unusual. This one sat on the doorstep, took off his boots and replaced them with carpet slippers from a suitcase. He also took out a white coat with the company logo on the back. He picked a clipboard, ruler and pencil from his case and said, 'Please show me the job.' She told me, 'I don't care if he has never wired a plug in his life: there is no way he will not get the job.'*

4.3 Image

1. We manage our image very carefully in our business.   [ ]

2. Our customers perceive us as we want to be perceived.   [ ]

3. Our image creates new opportunities for us.   [ ]

4. People say good things about us.   [ ]

5. Our image creates trust and goodwill with our customers.   [ ]

6. Our image supports our business objectives.   [ ]

Fewer than four ticks and you need to take *Action*.

4.3 Image

Action **Action 1:** Write down the image you wish to portray in your business. Use this checklist.

Your image covers
- *Name of firm*
- *Your name*
- *Address*
- *Personal appearance, clothes*
- *Car/vehicle*
- *Written correspondence*
- *Signs*
- *Logos*
- *Verbal correspondence, accent, self talk*
- *Where you are seen*
- *The way the phone is answered*
- *Choice of colour in your livery*
- *Quality of typing/word-processing*
- *Qualifications*
- *Membership of associations*
- *Associations with other parties/bodies*
- *Packaging*
- *Quality of paper and materials*
- *Personal manner*
- *Appearance of premises*
- *Spelling*
- *How quickly you respond to enquiries*
- *Ability to do what you say you will do – on time*
- *Type-styles on printed materials*
- *Quality of finish on printed material*

(You know what's coming next by now, don't you?)

Ask your key customers what image you portray. Ask them to do it in three words; this forces them to think. Take action on the results.

Action 2: Get an independent opinion on the image your stationery and livery give to the outside world.

Action 3: Try changing one aspect of your image and assess the impact.

Action 4: If you can afford it, employ an image consultant to look you over. What clothes and colours suit you best?

Awareness / The undiscussable side of business

There are difficult areas to discuss in business, so they often remain undiscussed. I call it the 'shadow side' of the organization. The shadow side is the culture, the politics and the social system within the business. The shadow side is all those things which substantially affect productivity and quality of life but which are not written down or discussed formally, and can dramatically impact on the future of the business. One of our companies described their culture as 'Dull obedience upwards, sheer brutality down.' So it was not surprising that when the managing director wanted his people to 'innovate and take responsibility' it did not happen. What are the war stories about your business? What do people talk about around the coffee machine?

There is no company that is run on purely rational business lines: the shadow side always intervenes. Here are some of the problems:

Problem 1: *Loosely coupled systems* This means the key aspects of a Hallmark do not support each other. Neat Ideas wanted their distribution system (key resources) to support their vision – 'most effective office supplies mail order company in the UK'. Once they sorted out their distribution resources it was coupled to the vision.

Often companies will try to develop new business where they do not have the core skills. Again, this is an example of the Hallmarks being loosely coupled.

Problem 2: *'Individuals'* Everybody is different, and their goals and aspirations may not always align with your business objectives. How do you get them to perform well? Leadership needs to be tailored to individuals' needs.

Our company had a super salesman who only wanted to work three days a week. Would you let him? He brought in 60 per cent of the business!

Problem 3: *'Politics'* Every business has its politics with a small 'p'. Cliques develop which can be positive or negative, yet they need to be managed. Some large companies have more politics and infighting internally than they do in fighting their competitors. An early warning sign is when owner-managers claim with pride, 'We don't have any politics around here, we are one big happy family.' Oh yes?

Problem 4: *'Culture'* Culture is the way we do things around here (even though we don't discuss it). It is how we behave collectively. It has been called the software of the mind. It is all-pervasive and controls everything, including the shadow side. It is formed by beliefs we hold about our business; it is transmitted to everyone, and forms the collective mind of the organization which distinguishes it from any other. Culture can be:

Overt: Beliefs spelt out in a mission statement. It is there for all to see.
Covert: It's these that are – *unnoticed*
                             – *undisclosed*
                             – *undiscussable.*

> **Example:** *The covert culture of one of our surveyed companies (which has to remain nameless – see how undiscussable culture is?) appears to be, 'anytime will do'.*
>
> *So quotes went out late, deliveries were late, reports never came on time. When we discussed this with people they said that there was no punishment for non-performance and nobody ever said anything anyway.*
>
> *The owner-manager was horrified when we told her. When we questioned her more deeply we found her style was 'delegate' (it was more like abdicate) and let people get on with it. Guess who established the cultural norm in that business?*

To change the culture you have to make the covert overt. Here is a map to guide your thinking:

	Overt	*Covert*
Enhancing your achievements	Celebrate it!	Surface it or legitimate it or leave it alone
Limiting your achievements	Challenge it!	Surface it; challenge it; replace it

Change in culture is messy. Many people can write a marketing plan but how many can change the culture so it becomes a customer-led business? Quality manuals are no problem but how can you get people to live and breathe quality day in day out? If you only plan for rational change you are almost bound to fail.

The positive aspects of culture are that it should be the way you control your business if you can get everybody believing the same things. That is why I believe clear communication of vision and values is so important. They make our beliefs overt so everybody has the chance to feel part of the business and its culture.

4.4 The 'Shadow Side'

Assessment

1. *We are happy with our war stories – they support our business aims.*　[　]

2. *Our systems are not loosely coupled.*　[　]

3. *We accommodate individual idiosyncrasies very effectively in our business.*　[　]

4. *Our social and political systems support our business aims.*　[　]

5. *We are good at changing our people's beliefs and values.*　[　]

6. *We work hard at making covert aspects of our culture overt where appropriate.*　[　]

Fewer than four ticks means you need to take *Action*.

4.4 The 'Shadow Side'

Action **Action 1:** Talk to people around the coffee machine. What are the 'war stories' about your business? What do they tell you about the shadow side of your business? Main war stories in your business:

1.

2.

3.

4.

5.

6.

Action 2: What do these tell you about your business? The next time you plan to change your business try to take shadow-side issues into account. It is difficult, but your chances of success will be multiplied tenfold.

Likely shadow-side issues   *Action to address these issues*

1.

2.

3.

4.

5.

6.

(Remember, if you cannot identify any they will probably hit you between the eyes half-way through the change process.)

Action 3: Get a third party to conduct a culture audit in your business. This will identify all the shadow-side issues for you. You cannot conduct a culture audit yourself, as you are part of the system. The audit needs to be independent, and will provide you with the basis for making your plans work.

Action 4: Review the lessons learned from the last time you tried to introduce change and it failed.

Step 1: Gather your people together. Discuss what happened.

Step 2: Ask the question, 'What *really* went wrong?'

Step 3: Talk about the politics and issues that were never discussed but affected the initiative.

**4.5
Changing**

Awareness / Staying in tune

There is an interesting conundrum that faces successful businesses – how to keep the recipe for success intact while adapting to change in their market.

Change in competitor activity or customer needs often provides the incentive to change the business, but what about when *we* want to change it? It appears that only crisis brings the energy to change; alternatively, a 'new broom' or change of leadership will hasten the change process.

The rest of the time, change is difficult. Tom Peters is right – emphasise quality, listen to customers, involve people, take dramatic action. These principles are confirmed by our own research. But those who preach the gospel of excellence do not deal with the deep-seated sluggishness of resistance to change that pervades most companies. It is an inertia that has been called the psychopathology of the average, a mouthful yet prophetic. We settle for mediocrity and do not change unless already forced to by external influences. Many companies in the UK have made this an art form.

Tom Peters' *Excellence* books provided a spur, and excellence became a destination sought by many. However, the world is changing too fast for excellence alone to provide a safe harbour. The trick lies in adapting the company to a constantly changing world. The challenge will never go away: 'getting there is half the fun.'

> **Example:** *The difference between getting there and the constant journey is epitomized in the quality area. BS5750 is the destination, an accredited standard – a document. However, the pursuit of quality improvements to products and services is a never-ending goal. It lasts for ever.*

So how do you stimulate change and make it stick?

Perhaps the most common cause of difficulty is that we underestimate the complexity of change. Change is a cultural process, it is not always rational. You need to change people's beliefs before you change their actions. This needs an understanding about how beliefs can be changed.

Your job is key to the change process in your company. You are the role model for others in your business. You need to spread your new vision to everybody, to act as a champion of change. Your people notice what you do and say, and so behave in a way which supports the change. Do you behave in ways that support the change you are aiming for?

Managers benefit from the use of a model in managing change effectively. Here is one used by a number of organizations that have successfully managed change.

Step 1: Assess the current situation

    a) *Assess problems and opportunities*
    b) *Examine 'blind spots'*
    c) *Select opportunities for action*

Step 2: Craft a new future

    a) *Develop a range of possibilities*
    b) *Select a new future*
    c) *Gain commitment to the new future*

Step 3: Making a plan

    a) *Brainstorm ways of moving from the current situation to a new route*

161

b) *Develop a plan*
c) *Make the plan work*

This process is well covered in the book *Managing Change and Innovation* by Gerald Egan (University Associates)

Successful businesses are in a state of constant change while maintaining the integrity of the core product and service. Change is a constant in today's world, but it starts with beliefs and culture, not statistics and procedures.

4.5 Changing

Assessment

*Tick here if this
is true for your
business*

1. *We look forward to and welcome change rather
    than feel threatened by it.* [ ]

2. *We are good at making change stick in our
    business.* [ ]

3. *Our managers are good role models for change.* [ ]

4. *We are not afraid to make mistakes.* [ ]

5. *We first change people's beliefs and then
    their actions.* [ ]

6. *We support change with symbolic actions.* [ ]

Fewer than four ticks means you need to take *Action*.

163

4.5 Changing

Action   **Action 1:**   Make change stick.

           Action 2:   Think about a change you want to make to your business. Ask yourself, 'How should I act as a role model to get the message across?'

1.

2.

3.

4.

5.

6.

Remember, what counts are actions, not words.

           Action 3:   Change something in your business meeting times, venues, dates, systems, anything. Sponsor the change and see what happens. Things I could change in my business:

1.

2.

3.

4.

5.

6.

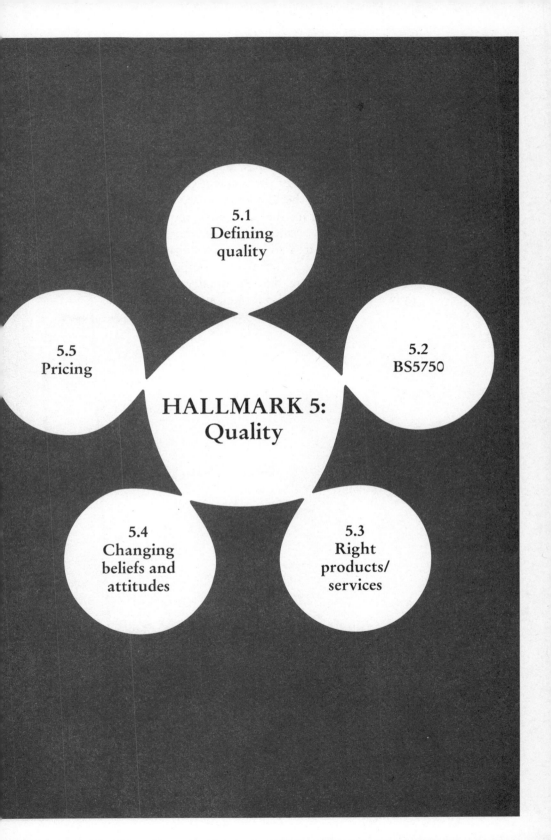

5.1
Defining
quality

5.2
BS5750

5.5
Pricing

HALLMARK 5:
Quality

5.4
Changing
beliefs and
attitudes

5.3
Right
products/
services

Quality is a key. It is one of the ways our successful companies compete, add value and charge premium prices. In their business quality is everyone's responsibility and is not left to chance.

Quality is everything in our successful companies. They are paranoid about it. They will do anything to uphold or improve the quality of the product or service. They instinctively respond to the challenge recognized by the top 250 European managing directors in response to the question, 'What are the key issues for the nineties?' The majority said, 'Coping with increased customer demands for product quality and service.' Successful companies intuitively recognized and responded to the quality challenge. This section shows you how to follow their excellent example.

Awareness / What quality really means

Many people talk today about quality using the buzz words TQM, SPC and BS5750. But what does quality really mean? There are two key facets:

Customer requirements: Does the product conform to customer requirements every time? Clearly, not all customer requirements are obvious or tangible. My partner was buying a dress recently and, after visiting the fourth boutique, in desperation I asked her what she was looking for. She replied, 'I shall recognize it when I find it.'

Customer perception: In most cases meeting customer needs is not enough. The customer must perceive that their needs are being met. Quality is what the customers say it is!

Example: *A managing director I know changed cars recently. Having been used to the service provided by Mercedes he was amazed to find he had to deliver his new car to the garage for servicing. The service manager insisted that Toyota had the finest electronic all-singing, all-dancing service equipment. The customer simply wanted his car picked up for servicing. Sometimes what the company see as high standards of quality (technical) may not be the same as the customer's perceived needs (an easy life).*

The lesson here is to make sure you look beyond your own technical excellence to the total customer needs. There are several attributes that contribute to people's perception of the quality of your product:

Performance: *Does the product work well? The Persil ads aim to demonstrate that the product works well: 'washes whiter'.*

Features: *Those qualities that supplement the basic product and add to perceived quality, i.e. my friend's car.*

Reliability: *This is a quality requirement, especially where downtime leads to problems. Superior Cleaning Specialists guaranteed reliability in cleaning BT systems at a time when BT was sensitive to bad publicity.*

Durability: *How long will it last?*

Serviceability: *This is important – perhaps crucial – but also the most subjective.*

Another way of defining the two-dimensional aspect of quality is:

– *fitness for purpose: will it do the job?*
– *does it include the intangibles which make it into a premium product?*

We need to be clear about what we mean. The death-knell of some of UK engineering was the pursuit of quality by providing excessive durability. Products were durable beyond customer need and consequently highly priced.

What does all this add up to? The issue is clear. You do not define quality, your customers do. It can be possible to have too high a quality (adding cost), particularly when price is of key importance to customers. For example, people will travel by bus, often taking hours on a long journey in cramped seats, because it is a relatively cheap form of travel. Quality is not absolute even though the trend is towards high quality.

Quality is clearly concerned with customer service in our successful companies. One of these defined their approach to customer service as follows:

We have a customer service triangle:

Service strategy:

Our vision is maintaining market leadership by delighting our customers. This provides a rallying cry that permeates the whole of our business.

Customer-friendly system:

We try to make it easy for people to buy from us.

Effective front-line people:

Our business depends on our front-line people, so we train them accordingly.

How do you manage quality of customer service in your business?

Example: *One of our DTI Enterprise Initiative manufacturing clients told us that his customer performance levels were as follows:*

- *Delivery lead time*   *5 weeks*
- *Delivery (on time)*   *80 per cent*
- *Customer complaints*   *Less than 1 per month*

We analysed his data and found:

- *Delivery lead time*   *10 weeks*
- *Delivery on time*   *38 per cent*
- *Customer complaints*   *10 per month*

*The problem was that nobody monitored and reported
against their standards, so the problems could not be
perceived. The owner-manager was only told the
good news, not the bad.*

5.1 Defining Quality

Assessment

*Tick here if this
is true for your
business*

1. *Our customers' needs have defined the quality
    levels for our business.*   [ ]

2. *We listen effectively to our customers' expectations
    for quality.*   [ ]

3. *Everyone in our business understands what quality
    means and how they can improve it.*   [ ]

4. *We have a clearly defined customer service policy
    that delights our customers.*   [ ]

5. *We cherish our front-line people to encourage
    them to provide high-quality customer service.*   [ ]

6. *Quality is our major competitive advantage and
    this allows us to charge premium prices.*   [ ]

Fewer than four ticks means you need to take *Action*.

5.1 Defining Quality

Action Action 1:   *Conduct an internal audit asking the questions:*

        Q. Does our product or service conform to customer requirements every time?

        Q. How well do we meet customer requirements?

    Action 2:   *Undertake a customer survey. Ask the following questions:*

        Q. Why do our customers buy from us?

        Q. How do our customers perceive us?

    Action 3:   *Get your key people together and discuss the questions:*

        Q. What does quality mean to us?

        Q. How do we constantly improve our quality?

**5.2
BS5750**

Awareness / The Recognized Quality Standard

BS 5750 is not concerned with specific product quality but requires that an organization implements and formally documents procedures that visibly ensure an effective and consistent approach to quality. Other standards which are identical are the European EN 29000 and the international ISO 9000.

Originally designed for manufacturing industry, BS 5750 (Part 4 1990) extends quality assurance to service industries, regardless of size or scope. The benefit from implementing a quality system to the BS 5750 standard accrues through accreditation by BSI (British Standards Institute): i.e. the formal approval by a recognized body that the company's quality system is up to the required standard. The benefits of accreditation, confirmed by successful companies in our research, are:

Registration	– *Provides an improved company image at home and abroad.*
Auditing by customer	– *Less likely because they do not need to check.*
Product consistency	– *Perceived as achieved.*
Quality system	– *Clearly present in the business in a formalized documented form.*
Monitored performance	– *Through internal audit and management review.*
Morale	– *Improved for everyone in the company because they can identify with the success of the system.*

TQM — *Objective measurement of performance in all operational activities with the whole company involved forms the basis of Total Quality Management.*

'There is no such thing as a free lunch' – just as true for the acquisition of accreditation because of:

Time — *It can take up to two years.*
Effort — *During that period you will take at least one person from their normal role.*
Cost — *Expensive in staff training and education; systems will have to be changed.*

But if you want to compete with the best it has to be done. Increasingly customers are demanding BS 5750 from their suppliers, and there are no short cuts. More than one company has tried to go straight to TQM without the underpinning systems of BS 5750 and ended in a mess. BS 5750 has to be the starting point for a quality regime!

Example: *One company in the North-East became the first in its area to obtain BS 5750. Initially it provided the basis for competitive advantage and the chance to increase sales. Competitors have now started to catch up but it is easier to get there first and defend than to try to catch up and attack.*

5.2 BS 5750

Assessment

*Tick here if this
is true for your
business*

1. *We understand the definition of quality in
    terms of a documented quality system, i.e. BS 5750.* [   ]

2. *Top management is sincerely committed to achieve
    third-party accreditation.*   [   ]

3. *Employees understand the significance to the
    business of introducing a quality system.*   [   ]

4. *BS 5750 is applicable and relevant to our
    organization.*   [   ]

5. *We already have documented procedures for key
    areas of our business.*   [   ]

6. *We never have customer complaints about the
    quality of our product or service.*   [   ]

Fewer than four ticks means you need to take *Action*.

5.2 BS 5750

Action Action 1: Compile a list of perceived positives and negatives of introducing BS 5750 into your business.

Pros   Cons
1.

2.

3.

4.

5.

6.

Action 2: Send for information about BS 5750; get a copy of the Standard and read it. Talk to BSI and your local DTI office, which will send you brochures galore.

Action 3: Contact the DTI – you may be eligible for a grant for installing BS 5750 into your business.

Action 4: Consult your local press to see what awareness courses are available to find out more about the Standard.

Action 5: Calculate some basic quality costs in terms of scrap/rework and resolving customer complaints.

Action 6: Talk to your customers. Do they want their suppliers to have BS 5750 now or in the future?

Action 7: Assess your current practices – how much of your business is run on what people carry in their heads, by custom and practice, both good and bad?

Awareness / The product that people want

What is the right product or service? This section aims to provide an insight into this question.

Derwent Valley Foods, manufacturers of Phileas Fogg snackfoods, are the right products in my view. Here are some of their characteristics:

- *Expensive-looking and tasteful packaging that is distinctive.*
- *Unique products – e.g. Mignons Morceaux, small garlic croutons a cut above potato crisps.*
- *Products made from natural ingredients without added chemicals.*
- *Products that are consistent.*
- *Products that cause friends to ask, 'Where did you get these from; I love them?'*

In summary, the range works well and delivers what is promised. If all products achieved this simple aim then it would be a big step forward. So the right product is one that works well and does the job. Other features, additional to the core product, may appeal differently to different customers.

One of the problems facing many independent businesses is that their products often have no outstanding features. As one put it, 'Our problem is that if you turn to Yellow Pages there are 22 other businesses listed besides us, so why should anyone pick us?' Exactly. Why?

A good product not only does the job and keeps its promise but it has a unique combination of features to attract customers in an increasingly competitive world. Why should customers buy from you? Does your product work well and keep its promise?

Our sample of thirty companies revealed that the major features that provided customer appeal were:

- *Unique products with unique features*
- *Quality*
- *Delivery (lead time and reliability of delivery)*
- *Customer service*

Do you have a good product with enough features to appeal to different customer requirements?

The right product or service does not last forever. It needs to be continually assessed and improved.

Example: *Honda. In one year they received over 150 ideas for improvement from every single employee. An enormous number to assess but over 30 per cent of their net profits in that year arose from continual improvements. Some target to beat.*

One of the perceived implications of having set up a BS 5750 quality system is the need to stick rigidly to it. Do not equate consistency with stagnation – the documented procedures are not carved in stone. As improvements are sought and made these are incorporated into a formally documented framework. The challenge is to maintain the consistent discipline and commitment to quality whilst constantly improving every aspect of your business.

If most businesses had to wait for the innovator in the boardroom to improve things they would wait for ever. Consider the numbers. If your business has four top people and a hundred 'workers' then the view is:

Four trying desperately to find new ideas to keep 100 people moving forward.

A hundred waiting despairingly for four people to tell them what to do.

This view of management's role is based upon the following assumptions which require questioning today:

- *People need an authoritative figure.*
- *People need rules, procedures, systems – i.e. control.*
- *The leader carries the burden for everyone.*

This might be summarized as a pre-1990 view. The world is changing and so must our assumptions about business. Successful companies are characterized by people who seem to hold different beliefs:

- *Flexibility and dynamism, authority.*
- *A sense of adventure and willingness to take calculated risks.*
- *Engagement and participation by all, leading to self-esteem based on competence.*

This view provides an agenda for the 1990s in a set of beliefs which turns the original equation on its head, hence:

A hundred individuals with the freedom to learn to grow and improve the business.
Four senior managers supporting and nurturing the hundred.

Which system do you believe will create the most improvements over time? Which system is closer to the reality of your business?

The traditional view of how a business operates in today's world is frankly outdated. It is my view that unless UK businesses can make the change we shall lose our role among the world powers. We cannot compete with businesses where every person is committed to making constant improvements. The Japanese exploit it to their advantage; they call it *kaizen*. We need to start with changing beliefs at the top, and if they can't be changed then change the people or hang out the white flag.

5.3 The Right Products/Services

Assessment

*Tick here if this
is true for your
business*

1. *Our product/service works well and keeps its promise to customers.* [ ]

2. *Our product/service has a range of features that makes it distinctive.* [ ]

3. *We understand why our customers buy from us.* [ ]

4. *We have no problems in making improvements to our business.* [ ]

5. *We get more ideas and innovations from our people than we can handle.* [ ]

6. *Our people constantly and continually add real value to our business through new ideas.* [ ]

Fewer than four ticks means you need to take *Action*.

5.3 The Right Product

Action   **Action 1:**   Get your team together and ask these questions: Do we have a product which works well and keeps its opromise? How do we know?

Action 2:   List the features of your product/service. Does your product have enough features to make it stand out from the crowd and appeal to a wide range of customers?

Main features	*Competitive Product Main Features*
A	B
1.	
2.	
3.	
4.	
5.	
6.	
7.	
8.	
9.	
10.	

Is list A more exciting than list B?

Action 3:	Talk to your senior colleagues to assess whether you have a 1990s or a 1950s world view. Discuss the results.
Action 4:	Try to assess the value of continual improvements in the past twelve months. A good target from our research is 25 per cent of net profits. If it is less you need to get started quickly.
Action 5:	Consider implementing some of our guidelines to create a new vision for the 1990s.
Action 6:	Celebrate a success publicly.
Action 7:	Set up a system for continual improvements and develop the attitudes in your people to make it work.

5.4 Changing beliefs and attitudes

Awareness / Helping people adapt

Why is it that in certain situations and surroundings we feel comfortable and become upset when these change? These are comfort zones and the comfort they provide is very real. Unless we change our beliefs and self-confidence and imagine ourselves in a new situation then we will tend to stick to our comfort zones. People feel comfortable with the tried and tested, the familiar habits and routines. They develop a comfort zone which allows them to maintain their self-esteem and confidence. Change throws them out of their comfort zone and weakens their self-esteem, so they resist it.

> **Example:** *Think back to when you started your own business. Remember how frightened you were? Recall how quickly you made things happen and achieved results perhaps beyond your expectations. It was probably hard work – you were out of your comfort zone. But on reflection did you learn and develop? That's the pay-off from extending your comfort zones.*

The key to changing beliefs and attitudes is to change our self-image first. We need to paint ourselves into a new situation, to picture vividly what it looks and feels like. Painting a picture is vital because as long as we feel out of place then we find excuses for failing. Once we have accepted this new image our creativity goes to work to make it a reality for us. It becomes an adventure, not a threat, so adventure is taking ourselves into new comfort zones safely.

How can you change beliefs and attitudes in your business? One thing is certain – until you change people's beliefs no lasting, meaningful change can take place in the quest for quality. The easy part is to write the BS 5750 manual. The difficult part is changing people's behaviour so that they eat, drink and sleep quality throughout their working day.

Your job is to paint the picture and explain where you are going. Describe the benefits. What will it be like? Will it be an opportunity rather than a threat? What's in it for your people? What vision do you have for the future? You want their help in inventing it. Make change an adventure rather than a funeral, make it a 'want to' rather than 'have to' experience.

In these ways you will help your people expand their comfort zones and embrace change willingly rather than feel threatened by it. You cannot force change through a business without casualties. The casualties will be your plans for change, because when people are forced out of their comfort zones they sabotage the threat. They reduce the pain and uncertainty by making sure it does not work.

Clearly, however, some people cannot extend their comfort zones so they may need to be changed.

Example: *When I told my people we were going to set up a factory in Hungary and I wanted volunteers to go out to set it up they nearly died. The furthest most of them had been was Majorca! We had to change some beliefs and attitudes quickly in order to take up the opportunity. We made it fun; going to Hungary now is routine; people volunteer. Chameleon Designs*

How is change introduced into your business? Is change an adventure in your business? Do you help people extend their comfort zones?

188

Assessment

1. *We have been very successful in changing beliefs and attitudes in our business.*   [ ]

2. *We paint vivid pictures of the changes we want in our business to help people extend their comfort zones.*   [ ]

3. *We have a clear vision which is communicated to everyone.*   [ ]

4. *We make change an adventure rather than a threat.*   [ ]

5. *We have been successful in gaining commitment and new behaviour towards quality issues.*   [ ]

6. *We find change fun in our business.*   [ ]

Fewer than four ticks means you need to take *Action*.

5.4 Changing Beliefs and Attitudes

Action Action 1:   The next change you make, try painting pictures for people and help them change comfortably.

Step 1:   Describe the change and the reasons for it.
Step 2:   Describe the benefits to the company and the individuals.
Step 3:   Describe graphically what it will be like, feel like or look like. Be enthusiastic about it. Consider getting some visuals made up, such as slides, pictures, and so on, to show the benefits.
Step 4:   Ask for questions and concerns.
Step 5:   Deal with concerns very carefully – do not dismiss them.
Step 6:   Keep talking about it enthusiastically as if it has already happened.

Action 2:   Make your next big change an adventure for everyone concerned.
Action 3:   Make sure everyone is clear and committed to your vision for the future of your business.
Action 4:   Ask people how they *really* feel about the proposed changes.

**5.5
Pricing**

Awareness / Reward for your Efforts!

All our successful companies charge premium prices. Superior Cleaning Specialists charge higher prices than their nearest competitor. Derwent Valley charge three times more than the price of a standard packet of crisps.

The message is clear: if you

— *customerise,*
— *partner,*
— *develop your personality,*
— *establish effective systems, and*
— *provide high quality,*

you can then charge high prices!

The reason is simple: successful companies provide what customers want, add value to the product, and develop a clear competitive advantage. Price becomes less important in this equation. If you give people what they want they will pay you for it.

So do you charge premium prices that reflect the quality of your business?

5.5 Pricing

Assessment

Tick here if this
is true for your
business

1. *We charge premium prices to reflect the real benefits we offer our customers.* [ ]

2. *We give people what they want and they pay us well for it.* [ ]

3. *We have a significant price premium over our nearest competitor.* [ ]

4. *Price is not a real factor in our customers' buying decisions.* [ ]

5. *Increases in prices do not affect demand for our product.* [ ]

6. *We work smarter, not harder, for our money.* [ ]

Fewer than four ticks means you need to take *Action*.

5.5 Pricing

Action Action 1:   If you have taken this book seriously and completed the actions diligently, consider putting your prices up. You deserve it.

6.1
Critical
information

6.5
Taking
action

6.2
Information
system

HALLMARK 6:
Systems

6.4
Key
indicators

6.3
Financial
control

All of the successful companies in our research had good systems, both formal and informal. Their systems added real value by providing good-quality information to enable effective decisions to be made.

This chapter outlines the process of creating systems to support you and the business.

All companies should have control systems. Some will be more effective than others. Our successful companies have excellent control systems but they also collect information to help improve the quality of decisions. They provide fast, accurate and relevant information so that people can take action to improve the business. They empower people through information. This section shows how to empower people to make better-quality decisions with the use of quality information.

Awareness / Information needed to drive the business

To see how the use of critical information supports successful businesses, let us eavesdrop on some discussions with two companies, A and B.

Company A
Q. *What are your customer service levels?*
A. I don't know really. We don't get many complaints . . .

Q. *What management data do you get monthly?*
A. How much we have sold. We plan to get management accounts this year.

Q. *What information systems do you have?*
A. Do you mean computers?

Q. *What key indicators do you use?*
A. Key what?

Q. *How do you know whether you are successful or not?*
A. That's easy. When we are inside our overdraft limit!

Company B
Q. *What are your customer service levels?*
A. We have five measures:

- *Four-week lead time for delivery;*
- *Ninety-eight per cent delivery within fifteen minutes of promised time;*
- *Ninety-six per cent delivery ex stock within 48 hours;*

- *All customer complaints handled same day;*
- *Customers can place orders 24 hours a day.*

Q. *What management data do you get monthly?*
A. We have identified the key information we need to run our business. This is made available to those concerned within five working days of the month end.
   It includes:

- *Monthly accounts by product/profit centre;*
- *Sales platforms;*
- *Customer services levels;*
- *Key financial indicator;*
- *Levels of repeat business.*

This is all the information we need to manage our business.

Q. *What information systems do you have?*
A. From receipt of customer orders right through payment. These are available instantly.

Q. *What key indicators do you use?*
A. We have ten indicators that take the pulse of our business daily. They include enquiries, orders, quotes, average order size, customer service levels, etc. This information is graphed and we can assess trends daily, weekly, monthly and year to date. We use this information daily to take action to develop our business.
   We could not run our business without this critical information.

Q. *How do you know how successful you are?*
A. We know daily from our key indicators.

Which company does yours most resemble, A or B?
   Every business has critical information that helps managers make good decisions; without it they are effectively blind. It must be relevant to the key business issues; reams of computer printouts are useless. Companies that rely

on historical outdated information are like car drivers doing 70 mph looking through the rear window!

How do you establish what information is critical? Here is our approach.

Step 1: Consider your customers. Why do they buy from you? What do they really want? The results of your customer attitude survey is the place to start.

For example, if quality and delivery on time were considered critical, your effectiveness on these factors become crucial to your success. So start with the key issues from your customer perception survey.

Step 2: Consider how you get business. How effective is your business-generating system? Measure it. It is critical if you are to build future business.

Step 3: Obtain key internal data on where the real costs lie. One company found that labour accounted for over 60 per cent of its costs. Consequently labour productivity and utilization were critical to success.

Step 4: Where do new opportunities exist? Where do you get information on customers, competitors and market trends from? This is again critical.

Example: *Neat Ideas has decided its key information needs are to provide data daily to every manager in the business. This allows them to improve the business daily. Their major competitors cannot assess this information until six weeks after the month end. Who do you think is going to be more effective long-term?*

6.1 Critical Information

Assessment

1. *We have clearly identified the critical information we need in order to continually delight customers.* [ ]

2. *We have examined how we get business and identified what information we require.* [ ]

3. *Our internal analysis has revealed our major cost areas and other key issues we need to monitor.* [ ]

4. *Information systems have been established to provide quick, accurate, critical information.* [ ]

5. *Critical information is communicated to people to enable them to make effective decisions.* [ ]

6. *Our critical information enables us continually to take the pulse of our business.* [ ]

Fewer than four ticks means you need to take *Action*.

6.1 Critical Information

Action   Action 1:   Analyse your customer attitude survey. What are your customer's key needs in priority order? What does this tell you about the information you need to collect?

Step 1:   List customer needs in priority order.

1.

2.

3.

4.

5.

6.

Step 2:   Decide how often you need to monitor how well you are meeting these needs.

Step 3:   Decide how to gather the information to collect and monitor the key customer needs – e.g. daily telephone sample for delivery performance.

Step 4:   Feed back the information to people who need to take action.

Step 5:   Use your information system to check that improvements have been made.

Action 2:   Examine how you get new business. What information do you need to gather to manage the business-generating system? Does this information encourage you to act before problems occur, or is your information so historical that it should be relegated to a museum?

Main sources of business	Information provided quickly: Yes/No	Do we manage this effectively: Yes/No
1.		
2.		
3.		
4.		
5.		
6.		

Action 3: Act on the results of the above analysis. Examine your cost structure – where are the major costs? Are these monitored closely, daily or at least weekly?

Major costs	Effectiveness of monitoring: Excellent/Good/Poor
1.	
2.	
3.	
4.	
5.	
6.	

Take action on the results of the foregoing analysis.

Action 4: Talk to your key people. Are they getting the information they need to run the business? Is their understanding of the prioritising the same as yours? Where are the blockages?

Information required   *Your team's view*
for our business
(your view)

1.

2.

3.

4.

5.

6.

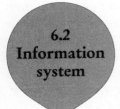

Awareness / Systems to enable decisions to be made

Most of our successful companies have good information systems, both informal and formal. Informal systems are established by continual networking and customer contact. Formal systems are computerized, providing key information quickly and accurately to decision-makers. This is a potential source of competitive advantage.

> **Example:** *If we know more about our customers' needs and our competitors' activity then we can compete effectively. Information is power in our business. Neat Ideas*

Accountants are often the instigators of formal information systems, so the financial data goes on to the computer first and if there is any capacity or interest then customer data may be collated.

It is possible to obtain excellent information systems off the shelf which are customer-orientated and fully integrated. Busgen, for example, is a customer-driven information system that fully integrates with the data and strategies set out in this book.

- *What information do we need to run our business effectively?*
- *How can we collect this information as efficiently and cost-effectively as possible?*

- *How can we set up a system that provides information when we need it (rather than, say, three weeks after the month end)?*

As a growing business DHP resisted investing in computers until we had to. Our greatest steps forward were made when we employed a full-time IT specialist fully to computerize and systemize our operation. I wonder now how we used to cope with little or no information.

My advice, from personal experience, is to computerize now and get your systems in as soon as possible. You will never regret it and looking back you may wonder how you managed previously.

During the research period we found that the less successful companies often spent megabucks on computer systems but: (a) they did not know how to use them; and (b) they were not selective about the kind of information to keep.

Does your information system add value to your business?

6.2 Information Systems

Assessment

Tick here if this is true for your business

1. *We have an excellent computerized information system.*   [   ]

2. *Our information system supports our key objectives.*   [   ]

3. *We have all the information we need on our customers, markets, and opportunities.*   [   ]

4. *We use our information system to make effective decisions.*   [   ]

5. *Our information system provides us with a clear competitive advantage.*   [   ]

6. *We are constantly upgrading and improving our information system.*   [   ]

Fewer than four ticks means you need to take *Action*.

6.2 Information Systems

Action **Action 1:**   Think about the key management decisions you have to make – e.g., price, priorities for expenditure, customers to focus effort on. Does your existing information system enable you to make these decisions with real confidence? If it doesn't, change it.

Key management decisions   *Quality of information available: Excellent/Good/ Poor*

1.

2.

3.

4.

5.

6.

Action 2:   Ask your key people whether they really have the right information to run your business. If not, do something about it.

Action 3:   Ask for an outside view. Do you use state-of-the-art computing hardware and software systems to support your business aims? If not, ask why?

Action 4:   Do you use a computer? If not, quickly book yourself on a course and get started.

Awareness / Sleep Easy In Your Bed

Successful growth businesses run the risk of growing out of control. This has been termed the Death Valley curve. The typical funds needed in a well controlled manufacturing company are about £25,000 of funding per every £100,000 increase in sales, whereas in a poorly managed company this can double up to £50,000 for every £100,000 in turnover. Turn your back on control for a mere few days, let alone months, and the cash requirements can escalate and sink your business. (A useful read on the subject is *The Genghis Khan Guide to Business* by Brian Warnes, Osmosis Publications, London, 1987.)

Not understanding the difference between cash flow and profit and the dramatic increase in cash required for growth can bring disaster. Obviously there are exceptions to this rule. Any customer who collects cash before delivering the service or any business that collects cash faster than it pays out may not have a cash problem. For the rest of us the Death Valley curve can be a real threat. The timing can also be problematic, as growth is usually driven by optimism and confidence.

Cash flow problems can pour cold water over everything. The first aim in financial control is to stay in business. This means managing cash flow, and understanding that gross margin – not sales – represents the true income of your business. It also means being clear about the breakeven point in your business – how much sales volume is needed to cover both fixed and variable costs? Breakeven is a key indicator and should be monitored closely.

> **Example:** *A colleague recently visited a small business which sold a technical engineering product that looked to have potential. The business had recently had a £400,000 cash injection. The team of £25,000 per year sales people was selling £35,000 of products in total per month. The bank was getting nervous. The break-even wasn't known and when my colleague made the calculation it was £85,000 per month! The bank was right to be nervous.*

The essence of cash flow management is good systems to control debtors and creditors.

All of our growth businesses have a full-time qualified accountant. Deciding at what point to recruit a full-time internal accountant is difficult. If your sales are £1m+ get a full-time accountant tomorrow: this simple piece of advice will repay the cost of this book many times over in the first twelve months.

If you have your accountant you don't need any more advice from me except this: he or she will have a different perspective on your business from yours, being cautious, pessimistic and careful, whereas if you are a true entrepreneur, you are the opposite – a risk taker. The point is that you need advice and help from someone with another viewpoint.

What value would an accountant add to your business? In my experience at least double his or her salary in year one!

Successful companies have the following:

– *Budgetary control*
– *Job costing*
– *Pricing policies*
– *Profit forecasts*
– *Effective borrowing arrangements*
– *Breakeven defined*
– *Control of gross margins*

Financial control is a mirror image of your perception of your business, i.e. the better you understand it the faster you

210

will want the key information. The less you see the need for good financial control information, the less you will understand your business. How do you see the need for financial information in your business?

> **Example:** *Financial control is vital to us operating in ten regional divisions in the UK. Each one is a small business and each manager has sales and GP details weekly. They send it to Head Office to let us know how they are doing. We control our business weekly. Ace Conveyor*

6.3 Financial Control

Assessment

*Tick here if this
is true for your
business*

1. *We understand the difference between cash flow
   and profit.*   [ ]

2. *We have adequate funds to grow our business.*   [ ]

3. *We have a qualified accountant in our team who
   attends and advises at all our important meetings.* [ ]

4. *We have excellent financial control systems that
   support our key objectives.*   [ ]

5. *We calculate breakeven and gross margins daily.*   [ ]

6. *We have an effective cash-flow forecast that
   enables us to manage our business effectively and
   avoid surprises.*   [ ]

Fewer than four ticks means you need to take *Action*.

6.3 Financial Control

Action **Action 1:** Employ an accountant full time if you don't have one – especially if sales exceed £1m.

Action 2: Produce a detailed accurate cash-flow forecast for the next twelve months. Employ an external accountant to produce it for you if you do not employ one and help them with the top line – the sales forecast.

Action 3: Calculate breakeven and gross margins by product/service and profit centre. Take action on the results.

$$\text{Breakeven turnover} = \frac{\text{Overheads}}{\text{Gross profits \%}} \times 100$$

(Gross profit = sales − variable costs)

$$\text{Example:} \frac{\text{Overheads £20,000 per month}}{\text{GP 30\%}}$$

$$\text{Breakeven} = \frac{20,000}{30} \times 100$$

$$= £66,667 \text{ per month}$$

Action 4: If you don't already have them, ensure you set good financial controls within one month, including budgets, cash flow, breakeven and gross margins.

Action 5: Read *The Genghis Khan Guide to Business*, by Brian Warnes, Osmosis Publications.

**6.4
Key
indicators**

Awareness / Taking the pulse

Key indicators take the pulse of the business on an ongoing basis. They monitor the important factors in the recipe for success for each individual business.

> **Example:** *We monitor the key factors in our business daily and report the numbers to all our people. We monitor average order size, delivery performance, out of stocks, number of sales enquiries, and cash received. These factors tell us everything we need to know about our business. Neat Ideas*

Successful companies decide what is important to monitor to maintain customer service levels. Less successful companies only appear to monitor internal issues, such as debtors, creditors, work in progress, and so on.

Where should you start with key indicators? Start with the customer attitude survey results. What did your customers want from you? Make sure you have a key indicator on the key issues raised by your customers. If delivery was a key factor, monitor it; if quality was key, monitor it. Factors that are not important can be left alone; it's obvious, really, but not many people do it.

For example, here are the key indicators from a successful company in a service business:

Quotations:	*Number sent*
Enquiries:	*Number received*
Sales:	*Value for week*

Customers:	Customer satisfaction rate – sample telephone survey
Finance:	Gross profit
	Cash flow

The business monitored these six indicators weekly. The Managing Director only requested to see four – the customer indicators, plus those not on target by exception. Each indicator was plotted on a graph; plan versus actual weekly, monthly, and year to date. He slept easy in his bed.

It is very often possible to develop six to eight key indicators that take the pulse of your business. The most successful companies focus on customer-related indicators.

> **Example:** *If we get the customer indicators going in the right direction and maintain them, the numbers in terms of profit follow as if by magic. Metro FM*

What key indicators do you need to run your business?

6.4 Key Indicators

Assessment

*Tick here if this
is true for your
business*

1. *We have identified our key indicators from a
   customer perception survey.*   [ ]

2. *We have a system for monitoring and reporting
   our key indicators.*   [ ]

3. *Our key indicators are effectively communicated
   to everyone in our business who needs to know.*   [ ]

4. *We have trends on our key indicators to monitor
   our progress continually.*   [ ]

5. *We take action as a result of our key indicators
   to keep our business on track and moving forward.* [ ]

6. *We celebrate success when our customer key
   indicators tell us, and fix things fast when necessary.*[ ]

Fewer than four ticks means you need to take *Action*.

6.4 Key Indicators

Action

Action 1: Conduct a customer perception survey, if you have not already completed one recently. Identify the key customer indicators for your business. Set up a system to monitor and report on them.

Key customer indicators	*Systems established*	*Effective actions taken*
1.		
2.		
3.		
4.		
5.		
6.		
7.		
8.		
9.		
10.		

Action 2: If you already have key indicators, check them carefully. How many customer indicators do you have? If none, go back to the previous action.

217

Action 3: Do you plot your indicators over time? If not, consider it. This will give you a good picture of the progress of your business.

Action 4: Check what happens to the key indicator information. What actions result? Who does what? Do things improve or change?

Assessment

is true for your

Tick here if this
is true for your
business

1. *We have already taken many actions suggested in this book.*   [ ]

2. *We have a culture of action in our business.*   [ ]

3. *Many different people have been encouraged to take action.*   [ ]

4. *Risk taking is encouraged.*   [ ]

5. *People are rewarded for taking actions that benefit our customers.*   [ ]

6. *Taking action is a constant process in our business.* [ ]

Fewer than four ticks means you need to take *Action*.

**6.5
Taking
action**

Awareness / Making things happen

The major difference between the successful companies in our sample and the less successful ones is the former *take action*. They do things, try things, and change things.

> **Example:** *There is a difference between knowing and doing. For example, at a seminar recently one of my colleagues asked the audience, Who are the most important people to your business? The response from fifty managing directors was instant and unequivocal: **Customers**, they almost shouted. The second question was, So if customers are the most important contacts for your business, how many of you have contacted them using a customer perception survey in the last twelve months? You've guessed the answer – none. Fifty say customers are the most important people, yet nobody does anything about it. If our seven most successful companies had been in the audience the answer would have been seven!*

There is a difference between knowing and doing, taking action rather than theorizing. The strange thing about business is that often people know what to do yet they don't do it.

One of the key purposes of this book is to motivate people into action to do things, hence the model

- *Awareness*
- *Assessment*
- *Action*

How many actions from this book have you taken so far?

Not only do actions improve or change the business, they indicate your intention to others. If customer service is a key issue and you jump in your car and take action on it, then this is a powerful message to everyone in your business. One of my business contacts put it bluntly: 'If you want to stifle your business then talk about it; if you want to improve it then do something!'

Start taking actions and you will get a domino effect. One action stimulates another and before you know where you are you're well on your way. Sometimes you need to do one or two simple things first to build confidence. Once improvements are manifest you become more adventurous, but make sure you keep control.

This book may have taught you something or may even have motivated you but the rest is up to you. The incentive is that if you take the actions outlined in this book your business will change and improve. However, the decision is yours, it's your responsibility.

Example: *An ex-boss of mine lit a candle before an assembled group of managers. He asked the audience to think the candle out; nothing happened. He asked them to plan the candle out; again nothing happened. He asked them to shout it out; nothing. Finally he extinguished it with his fingers. 'We can think and plan and shout about things, we can talk about them forever – but unless we do something nothing ever happens!'*

6.5 Taking Action

Action

Action 1: Examine your track record to date. What actions have you taken? Why? What actions have you avoided? Why? Try out some of the actions you originally avoided. What have you learned?

Action 2: Consider the section on systems. What is the most important action you could take to move your business forward? Take it now.

Author's Postscript

Well, that's it. Can I wish you the best of luck in making the actions work for your business? Remember, actions bring either success or learning.

Do not forget to use the Toolkits provided – they work!

P.S. I should be very happy to hear of your success and examples of making this book work in practice. I promise that if you write to me with examples and anecdotes I will consider them for the next edition.

David Hall
David Hall Partnership Ltd
Wadworth Hall
Wadworth
DN11 9BL

Internal Assessment Using a Structured Questionnaire

I suggest you conduct an internal audit of your people using a structured questionnaire. Here is how to do it.

Step 1
Photocopy the questionnaires on pages 226–56 and ask your people to complete them as honestly as possible. It can be interesting to obtain feedback from the various levels in your business ranging from yourself to your co-directors, senior managers, middle management and other staff, as applicable to your organization.

Step 2
Be ready to explain some of the business terms to people if they are unfamiliar with them.

Step 3
Analyse the results using the forms provided. What do the results tell you about your business?

1. Which Hallmarks are strengths (high scores) and which are perceived as weaknesses (low scores) in your business? As a guide, any score over 25 is high (maximum possible $6 \times 5 = 30$). Anything less than 15 (50 per cent) should be considered low. Low scores need action – they are potential disaster zones. High scores are strengths – but do not get complacent, make them better!
2. Are there differences in the scores between the levels of management? Why?
3. What actions should you focus upon as a result of this analysis?

BUSINESS ASSESSMENT QUESTIONNAIRE

Name: ....

Date: ....

Position: ....

You can contribute to the continuing success of our business by completing this simple questionnaire. There are no right and wrong answers. All you have to do is answer as you see it. Please keep in mind:

1. You should give your honest opinion – there will be no recriminations.
2. Answer every question.

The results will help us improve our business and we shall all reap the benefit.

Read each statement. If you totally agree with it circle 5; if you totally disagree circle 1. Use the scale of 2–4 to show your perception (e.g. if you neither agree or disagree circle 3 or if you do not totally agree but think there is some truth in the statement circle 4). If you do not understand a question ask for clarification or mark 1 as your answer. Only circle one answer per question.

1.1 Mission: A statement that describes what business we are in

		Totally disagree				Totally agree
1.	We have a clearly articulated mission statement that fits our type of business.	1	2	3	4	5
2.	We use our mission statement to guide our business decisions.	1	2	3	4	5
3.	Our mission describes accurately our true identity and what we are about.	1	2	3	4	5
4.	Everyone in our business understands our mission and finds it motivating.	1	2	3	4	5
5.	Our managers behave in line with the spirit of the mission.	1	2	3	4	5
6.	Our people find it easy to add value to our mission.	1	2	3	4	5
	Total score for Mission	....				

1.2 Vision: Spelling out the future you want

		Totally disagree				*Totally agree*
1.	We have a clear vision for our future.	1	2	3	4	5
2.	We communicate our vision to our people at every possible opporunity.	1	2	3	4	5
3.	Our vision energizes and provides an incentive for everyone in our business.	1	2	3	4	5
4.	We seem to find ways of moving towards our vision.	1	2	3	4	5
5.	Our vision changes as our dreams become reality.	1	2	3	4	5
6.	We are future-focused rather than being trapped by history (or how things used to be).	1	2	3	4	5

Total score for Vision ....

1.3 Core Skills: What you are fundamentally good at

		Totally disagree				Totally agree
1.	Our core skills are clearly defined, and we stick to them at all times.	1	2	3	4	5
2.	We are constantly trying to nourish and expand our core skills.	1	2	3	4	5
3.	Our customers confirm our own view of our core skills.	1	2	3	4	5
4.	We are good at developing our core skills into new opportunities.	1	2	3	4	5
5.	Our core skills give us a competitive advantage with our customers.	1	2	3	4	5
6.	Our core skills fit clearly with our vision for our future.	1	2	3	4	5
	Total score for Core Skills	....				

1.4 Environment: Scanning the environment for threats and opportunities

		Totally disagree				Totally agree
1.	We are very effective at monitoring our business environment.	1	2	3	4	5
2.	We are constantly identifying threats and opportunities to our business.	1	2	3	4	5
3.	We create more opportunities than we can handle.	1	2	3	4	5
4.	We have effective intelligence-gathering systems.	1	2	3	4	5
5.	We are rarely taken by surprise by our business environment.	1	2	3	4	5
6.	We feel we manage rather than are being managed by our environment.	1	2	3	4	5

Total score for Environment ....

1.5 Key Resources: Identify and maintain a supply of key resources

		Totally disagree				Totally agree
1.	We have identified and ensured that we have a regular supply of key resources.	1	2	3	4	5
2.	Our key resources support the focus and direction of our business.	1	2	3	4	5
3.	Our business will not be stifled by the lack of key resources in the future.	1	2	3	4	5
4.	We have made plans to ensure a continuous supply of key resources.	1	2	3	4	5
5.	Our people resource is well managed and adds real value to our business.	1	2	3	4	5
6.	Lack of capital will not limit our growth.	1	2	3	4	5

Total score for Key Resources   ....

2.1 Developing Customer Commitment: Every action taken considers the impact on customers

		Totally disagree				Totally agree
1.	Customers find it easy to buy from us.	1	2	3	4	5
2.	We do not employ any 'sales prevention' officers here.	1	2	3	4	5
3.	Top management sets high standards and provides good examples of our customer commitment.	1	2	3	4	5
4.	We are committed to understanding the differences between our customers' needs and wants.	1	2	3	4	5
5.	We can provide six good examples of our commitment to customers from our last month's activity.	1	2	3	4	5
6.	Customer commitment is a way of life in our business.	1	2	3	4	5

Total score for Developing a Customer Commitment   ....

2.2 Networking: Actively working with those who can influence your business

		Totally disagree				Totally agree
1.	We understand our network and how it impacts upon our business.	1	2	3	4	5
2.	Networking is a top management responsibility in our business.	1	2	3	4	5
3.	Top management spends enough time networking with key customers.	1	2	3	4	5
4.	We are not dependent on individual contact with key customers, we have many contacts.	1	2	3	4	5
5.	Networking creates more new opportunities than we can cope with.	1	2	3	4	5
6.	Networking is discussed and planned frequently at our management meetings.	1	2	3	4	5

Total score for Networking ....

2.3 Problem-seeking/Problem-solving

		Totally disagree				Totally agree

1. We are good at listening to our customers rather than selling them products.   1 2 3 4 5

2. We use problem-seeking/problem-solving as a major source of business generation   1 2 3 4 5

3. We help our customers identify real problems in areas for improvement.   1 2 3 4 5

4. We often surprise our customers with the speed and the effectiveness of our problem-solving on their behalf.   1 2 3 4 5

5. Our business is flexible enough to respond immediately to major opportunities.   1 2 3 4 5

6. We have well-proven procedures for problem-seeking.   1 2 3 4 5

Total score for Problem-seeking/ Problem-solving   ....

2.4 Customer Delight: Surprising customers with the level of service you provide

	Totally disagree	Totally agree

1. We have customer-orientated front-line people. 1 2 3 4 5

2. We create a high level of unsolicited repeat business by delighting our customers. 1 2 3 4 5

3. Customers often express surprise at the speed of our response. 1 2 3 4 5

4. We can provide six good examples of customer delight from our last month's business. 1 2 3 4 5

5. Customers' complaints are often turned into delight by the speed and quality of our response. 1 2 3 4 5

6. I have experienced customer delight. 1 2 3 4 5

Total score for Customer Delight ....

2.5 Market Development: The route to successful business growth

	Totally disagree			Totally agree

1. We grow by selling our proven products/services to more customers. 1 2 3 4 5

2. We do not waste major resources on diversification (unless there is no other option). 1 2 3 4 5

3. We plan for and allocate sufficient resources to developing new markets. 1 2 3 4 5

4. We only get involved in bringing new products to the market when there is a significant demand. 1 2 3 4 5

5. Long-term prospects in our primary markets are excellent. 1 2 3 4 5

6. We have an effective business-generating system to create new business. 1 2 3 4 5

Total score for Market Development ....

3.1 Structure/Roles: Adding value to the organization it serves

		Totally disagree	*Totally agree*
1.	Our organization structure supports our business plan.	1 2 3 4 5	
2.	Our organization structure ensures the right people stay as close as possible to our customers.	1 2 3 4 5	
3.	Starting from scratch and given a clean sheet of paper we would create exactly the same structure as we have right now.	1 2 3 4 5	
4.	We aim to build partnerships with all our key people.	1 2 3 4 5	
5.	Our business is built on partnership principles.	1 2 3 4 5	
6.	Partnerships are intrinsic to our business success.	1 2 3 4 5	
	Total score for Structure	....	

3.2 Customer Partnerships: Adding value to your customers' business

		Totally disagree				*Totally agree*
1.	The quality of our customer partnerships is our major business strength.	1	2	3	4	5
2.	We enjoy a high level of repeat business and referrals.	1	2	3	4	5
3.	Some of our key customers are our best friends.	1	2	3	4	5
4.	We aim to understand our customers' business better than they do.	1	2	3	4	5
5.	We add real value to our customers' business by working in partnership.	1	2	3	4	5
6.	We build partnerships by trying to understand our customers' customers.	1	2	3	4	5

Total score for Customer Partnerships ....

3.3 Staff Partnerships: Creating mutually beneficial contacts

		Totally disagree				Totally agree
1.	Our people give 110 per cent.	1	2	3	4	5
2.	Our people provide us with a competitive advantage.	1	2	3	4	5
3.	We operate on a true partnership business with our people.	1	2	3	4	5
4.	We have the right people to take our business forward.	1	2	3	4	5
5.	We have a clear set of incentives for our staff that encourage that bit of extra commitment.	1	2	3	4	5
6.	Our people take responsibility and produce results beyond our expectations.	1	2	3	4	5

Total score for Staff Partnerships   ....

3.4 Supplier Partnerships: Ensuring the supply of key resources

		Totally disagree			Totally agree	
1.	We have long-term contracts with our suppliers.	1	2	3	4	5
2.	We communicate our plans and requirements to our suppliers continuously.	1	2	3	4	5
3.	We treat our suppliers as we treat our customers.	1	2	3	4	5
4.	Our suppliers are an integral part of our business to the extent that they support our competitive thrust.	1	2	3	4	5
5.	We encourage our suppliers to develop in line with our plans.	1	2	3	4	5
6.	Our suppliers contribute ideas and innovations that help us develop our business.	1	2	3	4	5

Total score for Supplier Partnerships ....

3.5 Support Network Partnerships: Ensuring your support network adds value

		Totally disagree				Totally agree
1.	Our support network is clearly defined and well managed.	1	2	3	4	5
2.	Our support network adds value to our business.	1	2	3	4	5
3.	We make sure that we spend time with our families and friends.	1	2	3	4	5
4.	We are aware of, and have accessed, grants and expertise available to our business.	1	2	3	4	5
5.	Our bank manager gets regular information and contact from us.	1	2	3	4	5
6.	We are pro-active with our support network.	1	2	3	4	5

Total score for Support Network Partnerships   ....

4.1 Your Personality: Knowing yourself in order to understand your business

		Totally disagree				Totally agree
1.	I manage my time very effectively and act as a role model for our staff.	1	2	3	4	5
2.	I understand my own strengths and weaknesses and use this knowledge to advantage in our business.	1	2	3	4	5
3.	I behave in line with our business priorities by sending the right signals to my people.	1	2	3	4	5
4.	We have many symbols that reinforce our key business objectives.	1	2	3	4	5
5.	I have a clear set of personal values that guides our decision-making.	1	2	3	4	5
6.	We have undertaken psychometric tests in our business and use this information to build on strengths and minimize weaknesses.	1	2	3	4	5

Total score for Your Personality   ....

4.2 Business Values: The set of criteria used for making decisions

		Totally disagree				Totally agree
1.	We have a clear set of business values that guide our decision-making.	1	2	3	4	5
2.	Our actions are consistent with our business values.	1	2	3	4	5
3.	Our values are consistently adhered to by top management.	1	2	3	4	5
4.	Everybody in our business understands our values.	1	2	3	4	5
5.	We take account of our values when we develop our plans.	1	2	3	4	5
6.	We have a 'good' business that behaves with integrity.	1	2	3	4	5

Total score for Business Values ....

4.3 Image: The extent of your business external identity

		Totally disagree				Totally agree
1.	We manage our image very carefully in our business.	1	2	3	4	5
2.	Our customers perceive us as we want to be perceived.	1	2	3	4	5
3.	Our image creates new opportunities for us.	1	2	3	4	5
4.	People say good things about us.	1	2	3	4	5
5.	Our image creates trust and goodwill with our customers.	1	2	3	4	5
6.	Our image supports our business objectives.	1	2	3	4	5

Total score for Image ....

4.4 The 'Shadow Side': The undiscussable side of business

		Totally disagree				Totally agree
1.	We are happy with our war stories – they support our business aims.	1	2	3	4	5
2.	Our systems are not loosely coupled.	1	2	3	4	5
3.	We accommodate individual idiosyncrasies very effectively in our business.	1	2	3	4	5
4.	Our social and political systems support our business aims.	1	2	3	4	5
5.	We are good at changing our people's beliefs and values.	1	2	3	4	5
6.	We work hard at making covert aspects of our culture overt where appropriate.	1	2	3	4	5

Total score for the 'Shadow Side' ....

4.5 Changing: Staying in time

		Totally disagree				Totally agree
1.	We look forward to and welcome change rather than feel threatened by it.	1	2	3	4	5
2.	We are good at making change stick in our business.	1	2	3	4	5
3.	Our managers are good role models for change.	1	2	3	4	5
4.	We are not afraid to make mistakes.	1	2	3	4	5
5.	We change people's beliefs and then their actions.	1	2	3	4	5
6.	We support change with symbolic actions.	1	2	3	4	5
	Total score for Changing	....				

5.1 Defining Quality: What quality really means

		Totally disagree				Totally agree
1.	Our customers' needs have defined the quality levels for our business.	1	2	3	4	5
2.	We listen effectively to our customers' expectations of quality.	1	2	3	4	5
3.	Everyone in our business understands what quality means and how they can improve it.	1	2	3	4	5
4.	We have a clearly defined customer service policy that delights our customers.	1	2	3	4	5
5.	We value our front-line people and thus encourage them to provide a high-quality customer service.	1	2	3	4	5
6.	Quality is our major competitive advantage and this allows us to charge premium prices.	1	2	3	4	5

Total score for Defining Quality   ....

5.2 BS 5750: The recognized quality standard

		Totally disagree				Totally agree
1.	We understand the definition of quality in terms of a documented quality system, i.e., BS 5750.	1	2	3	4	5
2.	Top management is sincerely committed to achieve third-party accreditation.	1	2	3	4	5
3.	Employees understand the significance to the business of introducing a quality system.	1	2	3	4	5
4.	BS 5750 is applicable and relevant to our organization.	1	2	3	4	5
5.	We already have documented procedures for key areas of our business.	1	2	3	4	5
6.	We never have customer complaints about quality of product or service.	1	2	3	4	5

Total score for BS 5750   ....

5.3 The Right Products/Services: The product that people want

		Totally disagree			Totally agree

1. Our product/service works well and keeps its promise to customers.   1 2 3 4 5

2. Our product/service has a range of features that makes it distinctive.   1 2 3 4 5

3. We understand why our customers buy from us.   1 2 3 4 5

4. We have no problems in making improvements to our business.   1 2 3 4 5

5. We get more ideas and innovations from our people than we can handle.   1 2 3 4 5

6. Our people constantly and continually add real value to our business through new ideas.   1 2 3 4 5

Total score for Right Products/ Services   ....

5.4 Changing Beliefs and Attitudes: Helping people adapt

		Totally disagree				Totally agree
1.	We have been very successful in changing beliefs and attitudes in our business.	1	2	3	4	5
2.	We paint vivid pictures of the changes we want in our business to help people extend their comfort zones.	1	2	3	4	5
3.	We have a clear vision which is communicated to everyone.	1	2	3	4	5
4.	We make change an adventure rather than a threat.	1	2	3	4	5
5.	We have been successful in gaining commitment and new behaviour towards quality issues.	1	2	3	4	5
6.	We find change fun in our business.	1	2	3	4	5
	Total score for Changing Beliefs and Attitudes	....				

5.5 Pricing: Reward for your efforts

		Totally disagree				Totally agree
1.	We charge premium prices to reflect the real benefits we offer our customers.	1	2	3	4	5
2.	We give people what they want and they pay us well for it.	1	2	3	4	5
3.	We have a significant price difference from our nearest competitor.	1	2	3	4	5
4.	Price is not a real factor in our customers' buying decisions.	1	2	3	4	5
5.	Increases in prices do not affect demand for our product.	1	2	3	4	5
6.	We work smarter, not harder, for our money.	1	2	3	4	5

Total score for Pricing ....

6.1 Critical Information: Information needed to drive the business

		Totally disagree				*Totally agree*
1.	We have clearly identified the critical information we need in order to continually delight customers.	1	2	3	4	5
2.	We have examined how we get business and identified what information we require.	1	2	3	4	5
3.	Our internal analysis has revealed the major cost areas and other key issues we need to monitor.	1	2	3	4	5
4.	Information systems have been established to provide quick, accurate, critical information.	1	2	3	4	5
5.	Critical information is communicated to people to enable them to make effective decisions.	1	2	3	4	5
6.	Our critical information enables us to continually take the pulse of our business.	1	2	3	4	5

Total score for Critical Information ....

6.2 Information Systems: Systems to enable decisions to be made

		Totally disagree				Totally agree
1.	We have an excellent computerized information system.	1	2	3	4	5
2.	Our information system supports our key objectives.	1	2	3	4	5
3.	We have all the information we need on our customers, markets, and opportunities.	1	2	3	4	5
4.	We use our information system to make effective decisions.	1	2	3	4	5
5.	Our information system provides us with a clear competitive advantage.	1	2	3	4	5
6.	We are constantly upgrading and improving our information system.	1	2	3	4	5

Total score for Information Systems

....

6.3 Financial Control: Sleep easy in your bed

	Totally disagree				Totally agree
1. We understand the difference between cash flow and profit.	1	2	3	4	5
2. We have adequate funds to grow our business.	1	2	3	4	5
3. We have a qualified accountant in our team who attends and advises at all our important meetings.	1	2	3	4	5
4. We have excellent financial control systems that support our key objectives.	1	2	3	4	5
5. We calculate breakeven and gross margins frequently.	1	2	3	4	5
6. We have an effective cash-flow forecast that enables us to manage our business effectively and avoid surprises.	1	2	3	4	5

Total score for Financial Control   ....

6.4 Key Indicators: Taking the pulse

		Totally disagree				Totally agree
1.	We have identified our key indicators from a customer perception survey.	1	2	3	4	5
2.	We have a system for monitoring and reporting our key indicators.	1	2	3	4	5
3.	Our key indicators are effectively communicated to everyone in our business who needs to know.	1	2	3	4	5
4.	We have trends in our key indicators to monitor our progress continually.	1	2	3	4	5
5.	We take action as a result of our key indicators to keep our business on track and moving forward.	1	2	3	4	5
6.	We celebrate success when our customer key indicators tell us, and fix things fast when necessary.	1	2	3	4	5

Total score for Key Indicators ....

6.5 Taking Action: Making things happen

		Totally disagree				Totally agree

1. We have already taken many actions suggested in this book.　　1 2 3 4 5

2. We have a culture of action in our business.　　1 2 3 4 5

3. Many different people have been encouraged to take action.　　1 2 3 4 5

4. Risk taking is encouraged.　　1 2 3 4 5

5. People are rewarded for taking actions that benefit our customers.　　1 2 3 4 5

6. Taking action is a constant process in our business.　　1 2 3 4 5

Total score for Taking Action　　............

SCORING SHEET

		Score
Hallmark 1	**Focus/Direction**	**Score**
	Mission	--------
	Vision	--------
	Core Skills	--------
	Environment	--------
	Key Resources	--------
Hallmark 2	**Customerising**	**Score**
	Developing a Customer Commitment	--------
	Networking	--------
	Problem-seeking/Problem-solving	--------
	Customer Delight	--------
	Market Development	--------
Hallmark 3	**Partnering**	**Score**
	Structure/Roles	--------
	Customer Partnerships	--------
	Staff Partnerships	--------
	Supplier Partnerships	--------
	Support Network Partnerships	--------
Hallmark 4	**Personality**	**Score**
	Your Personality	--------
	Business Values	--------
	Image	--------
	The 'Shadow Side'	--------
	Changing	--------
Hallmark 5	**Quality**	**Score**
	Defining Quality	--------
	BS 5750	--------
	Right Products/Services	--------
	Changing Beliefs and Attitudes	--------
	Pricing	--------
Hallmark 6	**Systems**	**Score**
	Critical Information	--------
	Information Systems	--------

Financial Control   --------
Key Indicators   --------
Taking Action   -------

Total Scores
Hallmark 1   --------
Hallmark 2   --------
Hallmark 3   --------
Hallmark 4   --------
Hallmark 5   --------
Hallmark 6   --------

Grand Total   -------- (Maximum possible 900)

Ratings
Low scores, 0–300
    Urgent action required

Average scores, 300–600
    Take action

High scores, 600–900
    Prioritise actions

Customer Perception Survey

It is suggested that you conduct a Customer Perception Survey in order to address the questions set out in the assessment sections in this book. This is best carried out by telephone. The survey asks customers their views in a systematic manner. Here is the procedure, which is a tried and tested method.

Step 1:   Identify your key customers:

A)   Which 20 per cent of customers produce 80 per cent of sales?
B)   Identify some 'lost' customers (your key customers will normally give you 'good news' – you want the full picture).
C)   Identify some customers you would like to do more business with in the future.

Aim for 30–50 contacts in total (more, if you have a large customer base i.e. 500+).

Step 2:   Write the following letter to your contacts.

Dear X,

In order to enable us to evaluate and improve the overall standard of the service (products) we offer and to ensure that we meet our customer requirements at all times, we would appreciate your help.

To do this we need to speak directly to our customers to seek their help and advice on our existing service (product), and over the next few weeks we shall telephone you.

As a valued contact we hope you can help us to help you. Your views will be greatly appreciated.

Thank you.

Step 3:   Determine what information you require and design your questions. Here are some we have prepared:

Q   What do you look for in a supplier? (probe to get at their detailed needs)
Q   What disappoints you about suppliers?

Q What improvements could we make in our service to you?
Q What frequency of contact with suppliers do you prefer?
Q How could we do more business with you in the future?

Clearly you can design your own questions or change them into your own words. Each question can be followed up with probes to establish real issues. For example:

Q Can you give me an example?
Q Exactly what do you mean by that?
Q What other things are important to you?

Step 4: Decide if someone in your business is to conduct the telephone survey or whether to employ a third party.

	Pros		Cons	
Own staff member	*	Knows your business well	*	Inexperienced at surveys
	*	Can sort facts from opinions	*	Customers may think you're selling
	*	Cheaper	*	Customers may be guarded in answers
			*	May be biased
Third party, i.e. a consultant	*	Objective 'no axe to grind'	*	Unfamiliar with the nuances of your business
	*	Experienced in undertaking such surveys	*	More expensive

Step 5: Telephone the selected customers about seven days after the sending of your letter (Step 2).
    Set out your questions on a sheet of paper, leaving spaces for answers. Note the company's name on each form. Instruct the researcher to stick to the questions and to write answers verbatim – not to interpret the answers. Ask open questions. If the survey is conducted professionally and properly it will enhance your image with your contacts.
    Sometimes businesses express concerns that customers will not talk and/or will not respond honestly. Our experience with more than 500 customer perception surveys is that the problem is not getting customers to talk but to stop them

talking! Remember, they are more used to salesmen trying to sell them products than people genuinely interested in their views: 'We only ever hear from them when they want to sell us something.'

Step 6: Ask your customers to identify what is most important for each of the issues in Step 3. Then do the same with all the issues. Finally, take each in turn and ask them to rate your business on a scale of 1–5, with 1 = awful and 5 = excellent.

Example: 'Mr Customer, you said delivery was your number 1 priority. On a scale of 1–5 (5 being excellent) where would you rate us? Do you mind if I ask whether our major competitors are above or below that rating?'

Step 7: Assess all the information collected. What was the most frequently mentioned issue? What are your customers' needs in priority order? How is the company perceived?

You should end up with an aggregate list of customer needs and a rating of your performance compared to your competitors (see example below).

You can see from this example that such quality of information provides a much better objective assessment of your business than guesswork.

Clearly the next step is to take *action* to build on your strengths and address critical weaknesses. You may also have identified some new opportunities in your research which you now want to take up.

Example from one company participating in the basic research for this book:

Customer needs (in priority order)

		Company rating	Competitor rating
1.	BS 5750 Quality Assured	9	3
2.	Delivery on time	5	8
3.	Price	7	7
4.	Technical back-up at weekend	9	2
5.	Three-week lead time	3	10
6.	Local representation	7	6

Have a go yourself. What do you think they should focus on?

1.

2.

3.

4.

We would suggest:

1. Emphasizing quality assurance to new prospects.
2. Improving delivery performance to existing customers as quickly as possible.
3. Emphasizing technical back-up to customers, particularly outside the working week.
4. Cutting lead times to three weeks.

In addition, customers said the following about them:

	Percentage of customers
• Difficult to place orders out of working hours	60
• Do not see sales contact often enough.	40
• Only see people when you want an order.	30
• Never return our calls.	20
• Quick to respond to enquiries.	60
• No named contacts.	10
• No worse than competitors.	20
• They never listen to us.	15
• Average customer service.	40
• Good at technical support.	80
• Good at solving our problems.	50

What do you think they should emphasize?

1.

2.

3.

4.

Perhaps:

1.	Placing orders outside working hours	(60%)
2.	More sales contact	(40%)
3.	Return calls more frequently	(20%)
4.	Improve customer service	(40%)

Problem-seeking / Problem-solving

This is a process which you can use to build your businesses with either existing or potential customers.

Overview
Step 1: Build trust
Step 2: Storytelling
Step 3: Prioritize pain
Step 4: Consider possibilities
Step 5: Crafting an agenda
Step 6: Fix it fast

Step 1: *Build trust*
It has been said that the deepest human need is the need for respect. Respect is such a basic notion that it defies proper definition. However, it is certainly more than good intentions and 'have a nice day'. It is communicated properly by how you treat your customers. You build trust by:

- Showing respect for your customers, their time, their space, their products, and their views.
- Treating customers as individuals.

Respect means prizing the individuality of customers:

- Be warm within reason. Our research suggests customers prefer a professional, friendly relationship with suppliers.
- Disclose things about yourself. Show clients you are human too.
- Do what you say you will. Little things count. In the early stages of building trust customers' antennae are out searching for every scrap of information about you. Doing what you say you will build trust.
- Be empathetic. If they declare a difficulty, show empathy, not 'Sorry to hear your wife's left you but can I show you our new product brochure' (glancing at watch). You show empathy by listening attentively and feeding stories back to customers similar to those they tell you.
- Listen rather than talk. People like people who listen to their issues rather than bombard them with facts, opi-

nions, and the name of next door's cat!
- Ask questions rather than make statements. A g
  to start is:
  'Mr X, to enable me to understand your busines
  do you mind if I ask you a few question
  establishes the right to ask questions. Remer
  maxim: 'People make relationships, they do n
  purchases.'
- Be genuine. Admit errors and mistakes. Tell th
  all times, and never make promises you can't

This is how to get customers to tell their stories. *I*
problem-raising questions. Like this:

Supplier:	*The last time I saw you, Jim, you we*
	ling some new equipment. How did i
Customer:	Awful. It took three weeks insteac
	days!
Supplier:	*What was the problem?*
Customer:	Problem? You wouldn't believe it –
Supplier:	*Try me. We have just put some n*
	ourselves.
Customer:	(Tells story).
Supplier:	*What sort of impact did that have*
	business?
Customer:	(Tells story).
Supplier:	*What does the boss think about all t*
Customer:	(Tells story).
Supplier:	*If we could help you find a way th*
	situation, would you be interested?
Customer:	Would I?

Note:

1. The supplier keeps the focus on the pain.
2. Establish the impact on the business.
3. Find out what the boss thinks before tenderi

Sometimes you need to help the customer to und
severity of the problem before any energy will be
to solving it.

Step 2:   *Storytelling*

If a customer calls you and says 'I've got a problem, can you help?', great. However, in reality you normally need to go fishing for customer problems. Remember our maxim: Customers' problems = our opportunities. In order to identify real problems we need to get customers talking. Telling the story of their business, its problems and opportunities. There is a formula for determining the severity of any given problem situation:

Severity = distress × uncontrollability × frequency

The multiplication signs indicate that these factors are not just additive. Even low-level distress, if it is uncontrollable or persistent, can interfere with your customers' business. Your task is to help customers control the severity of their business problems.

Step 3:   *Prioritise Pain*

If you have done your job properly asking problem-raising questions and encouraging your customer to tell their story, you will probably have jointly identified a number of problems. Which one should you choose to solve first? There are two broad options:

- Challenge the blind spots
- Go with the flow

Challenge the blind spots   Sometimes customers can be too close to their problem to see the reality of their situations. They can become blinded to what is obvious to others.

When trust is built and empathy established you can carefully challenge their blind spots. The goals of challenging are to help customers to develop new perspectives on their blind spots. The responses to being challenged can come in various guises, so be warned:

- The customer discredits the challenge: if you don't like the message shoot the messenger.
- They devalue the issue: 'Well, it is not an important point anyway.'
- They agree but won't take action: 'I agree and I can assure you we are looking at it . . . '

Here is how to deal with these responses:

- Talk about problems they don't want to: 'Let's get it on the table.'
- Be specific when they are being too general: 'What is it specifically about our sales rep that upsets you?'
- Develop new perspectives on problems when they may be clinging to illusions.
- Develop goals and commit them to a new agenda: learn from the past. 'I know you had a policy of three suppliers to cover you in case of strikes in the past, but in today's climate how relevant is that policy?'
- Seek ways of advancing in the face of obstacles.
- Specify needs instead of a general hit-or-miss approach.

The key is to link your challenge to action: once they have seen a new perspective, try to get commitment to doing something. Chaotic action is much better than orderly inactivity. It brings learning if nothing else.

Challenging blind spots can be risky. It depends on the quality of your relationship. However, if you had a problem and a friend helped you clarify it, develop a new perspective on it and then resolve it, how would you feel about the person? A friend for life? Challenging blind spots is a skilled activity requiring counselling or consulting as opposed to selling skills.

Go with the Flow   Suppose that in telling their story your customer indicates that they think the problem is getting information quickly from suppliers (you). You see this as a detail, the real problem being the customer's specifications for your product. What do you do? Argue? Challenge? Fall out?

The alternative to challenging is simply to go with the flow – fix their perceived problem first in order to build credibility for tackling the real problem.

I prefer to work direct with managing directors to help them develop their business. Sometimes they perceive their problem as 'the management team'. It is clear to me that the MD is the problem. (At this stage the challenge is how to tell them and get paid!)

If it is a new customer I will have to decide whether to

challenge the blind spot or go with the flow. I would probably do some work with the management team, who are unlikely to be perfect (the MD's perceived problem), in order to build credibility with the MD before I tackle the blind spot and approach the real issue – the MD himself.

To summarize: (i) if you are uncertain or the relationship is new go with the flow; (ii) if you have a good relationship, have built trust and empathy, challenge the blind spots.

Step 4:   *Consider possibilities*

Having agreed on the problem to be addressed, the next stage is to *jointly* consider the solution.

Example: The customer needs faster, quicker information to enable him to plan production more effectively. What are the possibilities?

- Identify a manager to liaise with the customer daily.
- Use an on-line modem to send data quickly.
- Have regular meetings.

All of our research suggests that developing a feeling of responsibility for the solution in the customer is critical for the commitment to and implementation of the solution.

How can we create more options and new perspectives?

Step 5:   *Crafting an agenda*

Once you have agreed a possible solution or way forward, the next stage is to craft an agenda to achieve it. This again is done jointly with the customer. Who is going to do what? What is the timescale? Who pays for what?

We use the term crafting an agenda to indicate that most problems are unique, needing novel solutions. The quick fix, 'here is the answer, now what is your problem' approach rarely works in the long term.

Step 6:   *Fix it fast*

Whatever agenda you create, the magic in this process comes from fixing the problem quickly. This is particularly true if you are in the process of creating a new customer who has given you your first opportunity to show what you can do. Even if you agree an agenda time scale of one week, do it in a day. Surprise your customer.

Fast effective response is the key to success in this process of problem seeking and problem solving. Remember it was painful for your customer and speed is of the essence.

Problem seeking + Problem solving = friend for life.

The Business-Generating System

Introduction

The business-generating system is a sales and marketing system which combines information technology techniques with the style of marketing used by the fast-growth successful businesses. It benefits firms where there is the potential for repeat or referred business, where individual order values are significant and buying decisions are 'considered', not 'impulsive'.

IT in Sales and Marketing

The use of computer-based sales and marketing systems in business is growing at 30 per cent per annum in the UK. MSPs (marketing and sales productivity systems) provide the following benefits:

- increased sales
- more effective resource utilization
- automatic collection of market information

Research by Shaw Consulting in 1990 indicated that users of MSP systems expected a 7 per cent increase between 1990 and 1992. Evidence from research in the United States shows that early adapters of MSP systems gained sales increases of between 10 per cent and 30 per cent.
   The business-generating system uses the latest 4GL (fourth generation language) program which combines the benefits of database reporting and automation of administration systems management (hence time-saving) with user friendliness and adaptability.

'Relationship Marketing'

All of us are exposed to over 50,000 'selling messages' every year. The effect is that people are becoming hardened. The message from the successful companies demonstrates the strength of the caring and personal approach. The present economic climate has heralded the advent of 'relationship marketing', i.e. Hallmarks as opposed to technique-based marketing, involving problem-seeking/problem-solving, networking and friend for life.

The usual situation is that the top person in any firm is naturally 'good' at relationship marketing, either deliberately or instinctively. The barriers to growth usually happen when the sales demands begin to exceed the time availability of the top person. Stagnation and even decline result if the firm is a 'relationship marketing' culture and does not empower other senior employees with the skills and desire to use the technique.

Where the Business-generating System counts

The business-generating system enables firms to make the break from potential stagnation. The IT component makes time input more productive, resource investment accountable through live management reporting, and data handling easy. The underpinning philosophy expands on these benefits to provide a winning marketing formula for the 1990s which, while being numerate and monitorable, is a refreshing change from the aggression and impersonality that direct mailing or selling creates.

How the Business-generating System works

The success of the business-generating system is based around the following fundamental points.

Fits with your Focus/Direction

BGS does not try to impose on you new ways of doing things, but recognizes what works for you and builds on these strengths.

Focuses your Objectives

Included in the BGS is a marketing review to make sure business development efforts are focused and in pursuit of clear business objectives.

Links Marketing to Financial Targets

Using BGS, the volume and type of marketing activity is planned to generate the level of business needed to meet your financial targets.

Measurable Outcomes – Key Indicators

The computer database at the heart of BGS enables management to monitor outcomes from its investments and review key indicators on the performance of individuals, methods, products and the entire business. Quite simply, this means a visible business health, knowledge of the areas of real value, and the ability to use such information to stay ahead of competition.

Key Indicators

The business-generating system produces 'key indicators' to show management the health and effectiveness of a business. Note that these key indicators occur upstream of conventional financial indicators, thus giving firms forward visibility of financial performance.

Indicators	Purpose
Business plan indicators	Defined from the chosen plan, and used to track effectiveness of the plan.
Customer delight	Percentage of 'demand-led' new business, indicative of sustainable competitive advantage.
Working prospects value	Level of quoted business necessary to sustain sales platform at operational target.

Conversion rate	Barometer of change and marketing effectiveness.
Sales required	Order-book value to meet business plan objectives.
Sales invoiced	Determinant of production effectiveness in conjunction with sales platform.

Appendix: The Research Programme

Introduction

There are about 40,000 British companies which employ between 50 and 5000 people. In fact, 70 per cent of non-government employees work for enterprises (both incorporated and unincorporated businesses) employing less than 500 people. Reliable statistics about such companies are hard to come by, but it is estimated that this sector generates around 30 per cent of gross domestic product. There may be another million businesses with ambitions to develop their business.

Despite their importance to the UK economy, small independently-owned businesses receive remarkably little attention. Even in the United States, which celebrates its independent sector, they are the 'silent majority'. Also, they lack comprehensive and authoritative representation in the UK, either at an association level or in government.

The 1980s fuelled the growth of the private sector. Over the past decade there has been a net gain of more than 300,000 businesses registered for VAT, many of them tiny, but an increase nevertheless of nearly 30 per cent. Still, there is much to do if our independent companies are to compete effectively at home and abroad in a tough business climate with high costs of capital. What can be done to support ambitious businesses?

Clearly the support they need is different from that of the start-up enterprise or the multi-national corporation. What do they need?

Background   Alan Gibb and I were in a bar one evening swapping prejudices. We were surprised that we agreed on something (Alan is a professor at Durham University Business School and I am a businessman). We seemed to be asking the same questions. Is marketing taught in a way that is relevant to small independent businesses? Do small businesses really need to know how ICI develops marketing plans? (It is not uncommon at some business schools to find independent businesses being taught by bank managers, using Jaguar Cars as an example!). We wondered how:

- *independent businesses really grow (never mind the theory);*
- *we could support independent businesses in their development.*

These questions provided the basis for the research which eventually led to this book.

We decided to put my money where Alan's mouth was and sponsor some research. British Coal Enterprise Ltd and the Regional Enterprise Unit of the Department of Employment also sponsored the study. The objectives of our research collaboration were:

- *To find out how companies really survive, change and grow;*
- *To decide how we could most effectively support the development process;*
- *To develop some case studies of good practice which might be used by trainers and counsellors working with clients.*

Method of Research

The first step was to recruit a full-time researcher. We decided to go for somebody who was not a marketing expert (they may only confirm their own beliefs). We recruited a woman with no marketing background but a lot of common sense.

We asked our respective networks to identify some successful companies and identified those that fitted our requirement. These were drawn from the service, manufacturing and retail sectors and from the North-east and South Yorkshire to reduce regional bias. Eventually thirty companies agreed to be involved in our research.

The research was divided into three stages. The first was a fact-finding interview with the managing director. The interviews were recorded and transcribed. The first interview built up a factual company profile from forty questions. For example: What sort of company? How old? How many employees? How many products? Which markets do they serve?

Once this stage was complete and the interviews transcribed the transcript was analysed for critical instances. For example: 'We increased our sales that year threefold.' These were recorded for the next interview.

These interviews focused on the process of development identified from the first interview. How did sales increase threefold? The second-stage interviews were much more open-ended: trying to understand the real process of development. The interviews probed areas of real interest lasting 3–4 hours on average, and were recorded and transcribed (the transcripts being typically about 40 pages of A4 typing).

Going from a factual first interview to an open-ended one generated lots of data. Many questions that may have seemed naive to business people were asked by the researcher, who was trying to act like a sponge – absorbing information without any preconceived ideas of the answers. The use of open questions allowed the collection of qualitatively rich data. This method is a good way of surfacing real issues which might never get aired using a structured process. Each experience was unique.

After the second round of interviews we began to analyse the reams of data. We first looked for critical instances and blockages to growth. These were plotted on graphs against sales and profit trends. We went back yet again to the companies for explanations of the peaks and troughs. Why did sales increase here? What did you do to make it happen? We then classified the companies into composite groups, such as manufacturing and service, exporters and UK only. In order to analyse them (comparing and contrasting) we needed to establish criteria for success against which to assess our companies. What is success? How can it be defined?

We considered many aspects, like turnover per employee and capital expenditure per head. We finally decided on growth by number of employees and number of years trading. We defined success as those trading less than ten years employing more than one hundred people with a consistent profit and sales record. We feel this is defensible, given our original hypotheses. Clearly other people will want to use different success criteria – there is no unique answer.

We found in our analysis of the results that the seven really fast-growth companies had many things in common, not least the type of managing director. Our researcher commented that if she shut her eyes in the seven companies she could be talking to any one of them. Their beliefs, attitudes and behaviour were almost identical! We found that the process by which they developed was also remarkably similar. They all have the same Hallmarks. Hence this book.

Both Alan Gibb and I believe the research has gone some way to challenge the traditional textbook marketing based on large company models. But we are biased. Judge for yourself.

For those of you wanting more details of the research process contact Dinah Bennett at Durham University Business School, Mill Lane, Durham, DH1 3LB.

Ha
F
Di

Hallmark 6
Systems

Suc
Bu
Deve

Hallmark 5
Quality

Ha
Per